MW00423294

Crosscurrents

Navigating the Turbulent Politics of the Right
During the Horthy Era in Hungary, 1920-1944

Yakov Merkin

Copyright ©2017 by Yakov Merkin

Cover design copyright ©2017 by Miryam Merkin

Formatting by Polgarus Studio

All rights reserved. This book or any portion thereof may not be reproduced or used in any manner whatsoever without the express written permission of the publisher except for the use of brief quotations in a book review.

ACKNOWLEDGEMENTS

As I complete my Master's thesis and conclude my time in college, I would like to express my gratitude to the many people who made this possible. First and foremost, I must thank Professor Thomas Ort, who in addition to being my thesis advisor, is the reason I grew interested in the topic I have come to write about. Throughout the process of creating first the prospectus and then the thesis, Professor Ort has managed a perfect balance of providing guidance and feedback while allowing me the freedom to write the thesis I wanted to write. I would also like to thank Professor Joel Allen, who played a major role in my eventual decision to first apply to, then join Queens College's History MA program. Additionally, I will acknowledge all of my professors of history, both undergraduate and graduate, at both Queens College and City College, for providing great experiences and furthering my desire to first major in history, then go for the Master's; I can safely say that between both departments, I never had a bad instructor.

I also express gratitude to my family, which has supported me throughout my educational career; my grandfather, William Merkin, and my late grandmother, Doris Merkin, who financially supported my college education, and of course, my parents, Linda and Serge Merkin, who in addition to general support served as first readers for many of the numerous papers I've written over the years as a history student.

Contents

CHAPTER 3: OVER THE PRECIPICE: THE SECOND WORLD WAR

CONCLUSION

Preface

I first chose to research and write about the Horthy era in Hungary simply because I found it fascinating when I first learned a bit about it in one of my final undergraduate classes, and I also hoped (and still hope) to one day write historical fantasy set in that period. What I did not expect was for this topic to suddenly become relevant again, beyond Hungary (with the rise of Jobbik, as I mention briefly in the paper, Horthy and the general era in which he was in power has been a more discussed, controversial issue in Hungary since the fall of communism in the 1990s.) Specifically, this began with the accusations lobbed at Sebastian Gorka, an advisor to United States President Donald Trump, and who is of Hungarian origin. To briefly summarize the alleged controversy, at an official event several months ago, Gorka wore a pin that had the emblem of the Hungarian *Vitezi Rend* (Order of Heroes). Immediately, he, and the group, were accused of being Nazis and antisemites. Gorka's personal record speaks for itself, and makes the accusations made against him laughable, but I have even seen articles in which Gorka is given a fair shake where Horthy is referred to blankly as a fascist or a "Nazi ally," and his whole administration labeled as blanketly evil, with *Vitezi Rend* being directly linked to Nazism and fascism. This accusation is patently false as well, as *Vitezi Rend* predated Nazism, and while it did have antisemitic, pro-Nazi members, it similarly had members who helped save Jews. It was only after the war that it was linked to the Nazis, as any organizations at all linked to the Hungarian government were broadly labeled as such and disbanded.

However, more troubling to me is the high amount of things people (primarily Americans) get so wrong when writing or talking about Horthy and his administration, which, as this paper will show, was not a simple or static thing. I believe, however, that many of these wrong or oversimplified statements are made due to people's lack of knowledge on this topic, which I am certain is never covered in any broad courses on modern European history, and of which there is a very limited selection of English-language sources on the topic.

Just as Horthy is maligned today, so is Hungary's current prime minister, who is one of few European leaders who genuinely cares about preserving his people and culture, something Horthy would definitely have approved of. Viktor Orban and his administration have been attacked by many of the same people who attacked Gorka and, while this paper may not change those people's minds, I think it can somewhat enlighten them, and provide a more objective look at the Horthy era.

Thus, I am choosing to release this thesis to the public, at as low a cost as possible, in the hope that it will serve as an entry point for people to learn about and come to understand this fascinating period of history, as well as how some of what led to and influenced it informs Hungarian politics to this very day. I hope you will find it interesting, and that you will learn something about a criminally under-studied topic.

Yakov Merkin
Haifa
July, 2017

Setting the Stage

In May 2012, a statue of Miklos Horthy, Hungary's leader from 1920 to 1944, was erected in the village of Kereki—the first in what has become a series of statues and busts erected in recent years. Mere hours later, in the middle of the night, an activist smeared the statue with red paint and hung a sign on it that read, "war criminal." When later interviewed, the perpetrator stated unequivocally that he did not regret his actions. In recent years, the far right Jobbik party has been gaining influence in Hungary (and has spearheaded the resurgence of Horthy as a heroic national figure), and more recently, Hungary has been among the few European countries to close its borders to (primarily Muslim) migrants, citing a need to protect Hungary's status as a "Christian nation," rhetoric that harkens back to early twentieth century Hungary. These events, and the re-emergence of the name Horthy, make understanding the controversial period from 1920 to 1944 all the more relevant, if not simply for understanding the history, but also to understand the evolving Hungarian political landscape.

First, who was Miklos Horthy? A relatively unknown figure outside of Hungary and certainly the West, Horthy's career spanned a tumultuous period in Europe, in positions ranging from aide-de-camp of Emperor Franz Joseph, to captain and then admiral of the Austro-Hungarian Navy, to Regent of Hungary. He occupied a strange place as an old world man in a new age. Critics call him a fascist, a Hitler ally and an antisemite, while supporters call him a patriot, a hero, and the savior of the Jews of Budapest. As a result, his legacy is a hotly debated topic, especially in Hungary, ever since it emerged from under communist domination.

The aim of this study will be to take a look at the entirety of the Horthy Era, utilizing the available sources to not only analyze Horthy and his close associates, but also the political development of the larger Hungarian community which, as we will see, did not always align with Horthy's worldview. Utilizing multiple sources, including some which were published recently enough that previous studies could not make use of them, we will see that there was, indeed, a great divide between Horthy's conservative elite and many other segments of Hungarian society, which subscribed to a far more radical right-wing ideology over the course of his quarter century in office. While both the aristocratic conservatives and the new far right were of the right, they were separated by a key difference. The conservatives sought to maintain as much of the old order as possible, and in doing so saw the world through a class based lens. The far right, on the other hand, sought change as radical as that of the communists, if with a nationalistic bent. They viewed people through a race based lens. We will later see the different outcomes of both philosophies very clearly regarding the issue of antisemitism; both groups could be described as such, but what that meant and what they did would differ significantly.

Second, why take a look at this relatively obscure piece of history? There are several reasons that this topic, rarely discussed outside of Hungary, deserves another look. The first, a more strictly historical reason, is to take a look at this period, utilizing new sources, to address the debate surrounding the subject, to take a modern look at the Horthy era while not imposing contemporary values and ways of thinking on people born before the start of the twentieth century. Already, there have been several notable shifts in how Horthy and his time in office have been viewed. Views on the Horthy era have diverged based primarily on two factors: the political affiliation and geographic location of the people discussing the history.

It should come as no surprise that those affiliated with the left, especially the far left, hold Horthy and his administration in a very negative light. This judgment began as early as Horthy's rise to power amidst the overthrow of a communist regime. However, for the purposes of this analysis, it is post-World War II views, looking back on the Horthy era as a piece of history, that are most relevant. While there is not a great amount of research done on Horthy's treatment in historiography, a master's thesis written by one Charles Vesei summarizes the varying trends, ending in the 1990s. In Hungary itself, Vesei finds a clear trend. The historians writing closer to the end of the war display far more of a left-wing bias, both because they were not well trained and because they, as communist activists during the Horthy period, had come into direct conflict with the regime. Later on, as Hungary's communist regime grew less and less restrictive, historians began to approach the study of Horthy with more objectivity, though still with a left-wing bias. However, a sign of the shift toward more objectivity is that, for the most part, even critical historians no longer refer to Horthy and his administration as "fascist." A similar trend was seen in all countries in the Soviet sphere, as well as in leftist circles elsewhere.[1]

In the West, Horthy was generally viewed more favorably. Though there was some strong criticism, this was primarily during the later years of the war, when Hungary was, officially, an enemy of the West. Historians, including the British C. A. Macartney, held a more balanced view of Horthy, not avoiding criticism but generally painting a more positive picture, giving Horthy more credit than his Hungarian counterparts at the time. On the other hand, there was also a counterpoint to the biased critical accounts of Horthy by the left, as in at least one work (that is not considered scholarly) Horthy is portrayed in a nearly completely positive light. This book, *A Kormanyzo, Horthy Miklos* [The Regent, Miklos Horthy], was authored by Peret Gosztonyi, who lived in the West but had grown up in Hungary and had participated in the 1956 revolution. His book, the first serious attempt as a biography of Horthy, comes close to hagiography, something that is not helped by its lack of scholarly backing. It would not be until American Thomas Sakmyster, who first began writing about the Horthy era in the 1980s and published his scholarly biography of Horthy in 1994, that a

---

[1] Charles P. Vesei, "The Image of Admiral Horthy in Historiography," (master's thesis, Indiana University, 1994), 9-30; N. F. Dreisziger, "Miklos Horthy and the Second World War: Some Historiographical Perspectives," *Hungarian Studies Review*, XXIII, no. 1 (Spring 1996), 5-6.

standard seemed to be set regarding how to approach Horthy and his time in office. Sakmyster's book has since become possibly the most important book yet written on Horthy, and earns high praise from many other significant historical authorities (more will be said on his book later, as it plays a significant role in this thesis.[2]

Beyond contributing to the relatively limited scholarly work done on the Horthy era, there is another compelling reason to take a look at the Horthy era: Understanding modern Hungary. Horthy's legacy looms large in today's Hungary, with parties ranging from the right-wing Fidesz to the far-right Jobbik taking part in paying tribute to Horthy, sanitizing his image, some allege. This began with Horthy's reburial in 1993, and continues to this day with busts and statues being set up in Hungary. Beyond dealing with Horthy's legacy, however, understanding interwar Hungary helps us better understand Hungary's stance on the European migrant crisis today. While in the 1920s, socialism was seen as the major external threat that Christian Hungary had to defend against (and as a side effect, levels of antisemitism increased), today that threat is Muslim immigration/migration. Anti-immigrant sentiment, fueled by parties like Jobbik, has been growing (and we have seen more antisemitism as a side effect again), as well as an emphasis on Hungary's Christian character and its role as a defender of "Christian Europe." Just recently, Prime Minister Viktor Orban made a speech in which he called for resistance to pressure by the European Union to admit more migrants, citing, among other things, a need to defend Hungary's culture and Christian traditions. As we will see when we look at the Horthy era, this is not a new idea; it has driven Hungary, for good or ill, both in the past and present. The key for modern Hungary will be to ensure that the mistakes of the Horthy era, the populace's slide from the conservative Christian right to the far right, toward fascism, does not happen again.[3]

Finally, in the decades since the Horthy regime was ousted by Nazi

---

[2] Vesei, 31-46; Dreisziger, "Historiographical Perspectives," 7-14.
[3] Vesei, 47-52; Vlad Tepesblog, "Orban's Historic Speech Puts Hungary on War Footing," (Youtube video, 13:02, March 18 2016) https://www.youtube.com/watch?v=EbINrdyAXlE.

Germany, most opinions on it have fallen into two extremes: that of the communists, who termed it far-right, fascist, and malign it, and the modern Hungarian right, which considers Horthy a heroic figure and his time in power a period worth emulating. Looking at the evidence, however, shows that the Horthy regime falls in between these two extremes, and this paper will endeavor to show that while Horthy was far from perfect, and there is much to criticize, his administration was not a fascist one, and that Horthy himself was not simply a "Hitler ally," as many claim to this day. Horthy's Hungary, particularly from the growth of German influence in the 1930s through the Second World War, is an exceedingly complex and fascinating piece of history that deserves a fair analysis, one which does not attempt to impose contemporary values and ideas on an early twentieth-century society ruled by a man who, to his dying day, truly belonged in the nineteenth century.

To accomplish this, I will analyze the period chronologically, making use of what English language sources on the topic can be found, including works by eminent historians including C. A. Macartney, Istvan Deak, Nandor Dreisziger, Randolph Braham, Paul Hanebrink, and Thomas Sakmyster. Their historical texts span decades, with Macartney's work first published in the 1960s, and Sakmyster's in the 1990s.

The secondary sources that will serve as the backbone for this analysis will largely be the books by Dreisziger, Sakmyster, Hanebrink, and Braham.

Dreisziger, who held a Ph.D and earned official awards from Hungary for his work, lived in Canada but was of Hungarian descent, and published *Hungary's Way to World War II* in 1968, which is one of few histories of interwar Hungary written before the 1990s, and importantly for the purposes of this paper, focuses on the interwar period, with a focus on how Hungary entered World War II in the manner that it did. While it does not cover the war itself—and thus avoids having to discuss the years of the Horthy era that arguably are the most controversial—it does an admirable job of describing the political developments throughout the period.[4]

---

[4] Nandor Dreisziger, *Hungary's Way to World War II* (Astor Park, FL: Danubian Press Inc, 1968), 7-12.

One of Dreisziger's stated goals is to refute the claims of the communist historians of his day, who labeled Horthy and his administration as solidly sympathetic to fascism, if not outright fascist itself. Dreisziger portrays Horthy's Hungary as, ultimately, a country that struggled to find its place in the new Europe after the First World War, but ultimately was conquered diplomatically by Germany despite its best efforts to limit German influence in the region.[5]

Thomas Sakmyster's seminal, highly regarded biography of Miklos Horthy, *Hungary's Admiral on Horseback: Miklos Horthy, 1918-1944*, is one of the premier works on both Horthy and his time in office, and will be drawn on heavily in the writing of this thesis. Sakmyster, who was able to approach the subject as someone with no direct tie to the Horthy controversy (Sakmyster is of Hungarian background, but distantly; his grandparents moved to the United States well before the Horthy era, and he is a second generation Hungarian American, only learning Hungarian while in college) shows no bias toward of a man he describes as a fascinating, and flawed, figure; a sort of ideological hybrid, mixing nineteenth century conservatism and twentieth century right-wing radicalism. Horthy seemed, according to Sakmyster, to have lacked the skills generally make an effective leader, and yet he remained in office for twenty-four years. He was a self-professed antisemite and came into power on the heels of a "white terror"[6] that had antisemitic undertones, but did more to protect the Jews of Hungary than most of his European counterparts by not bowing to German pressure to deport them. He was a fierce anticommunist, yet eventually brokered a (failed) deal to surrender to the Soviets. These seeming paradoxes make him difficult to pin down as a man, and belies the simple descriptions of many of his critics, as Sakmyster illustrates.[7]

---

[5] Dreisziger, 61.

[6] The White Terror, which took place during the counter-revolution, was in essence an attempt to purge the remaining communists and get revenge for the Red Terror perpetuated by the communist regime, and was at least as bloody.

[7] Thomas Sakmyster, *Hungary's Admiral on Horseback: Miklos Horthy, 1918-1944* (Boulder, CO: East European Monographs, 1994), *v-viii.*

Hungary's Admiral on Horseback is no hagiography, and Sakmyster does not shy away from criticism of Horthy and his government, such as his involvement in the German invasion of Yugoslavia, which Sakmyster describes as Horthy twisting his sense of honor to justify reclaiming territory. At the same time, however, he points out the more admirable qualities of the man and his actions. His driving goal was to do what was best for Hungary, in his view reclaiming what lost territory was possible while still maintaining the country's freedom of action and his own sense of honor.[8]

Ultimately, Sakmyster paints an image of a flawed person, who was neither a hero, as the modern Hungarian far right argues, nor a monster, as communist historians have long alleged. Perhaps the best indication of the significance of Sakmyster's book is that it is seen as a valuable and reliable accounting of Horthy by significant figures in the realm of Hungarian history by historians who fall into both sides of the debate, such as Istvan Deak and Randolph Braham.

A book which was a later addition to the materials used in this study is Paul Hanebrink's *In Defense of Christian Hungary: Religion, Nationalism, and Antisemitism, 1890-1944.* Though it might not seem directly relevant to a study of the Horthy era despite covering the years of his administration—and indeed, Horthy is only occasionally mentioned in the book—*In Defense of Christian Hungary* provides a crucial angle to this analysis that most other sources on the period do not discuss in detail: the role of religion in defining the nature of Hungarian culture and the place of Christianity in the development of Hungarian nationalism, starting during the First World War and continuing until World War II. Additionally, Hanebrink pays careful attention to the trends of antisemitism among the different religious groups throughout his period of study.[9]

Hanebrink shows the development of the greater Hungarian mindset throughout this important period, something distinct from the political maneuverings of the Horthy regime but also something that most definitely

---

[8] Sakmyster, 385-387.
[9] Paul A. Hanebrink, *In Defense of Christian Hungary: Religion, Nationalism, and Antisemitism, 1890-1944* (Ithaca, NY: Cornell University Press, 2006), 1-6.

had an effect not just on policy but on the individuals in the Horthy administration. Horthy and his associates did not exist in a vacuum, and *In Defense of Christian Hungary* (along with other, more narrow sources) shows that the prevailing feelings among the populace played a not insignificant role in Hungary's eventual fate during the Second World War.

The final book I touch on here is Randolph Braham's *The Politics of Genocide: The Holocaust in Hungary*. Braham, one of the most well known experts on the Holocaust in Hungary, serves a role here beyond simply that of an excellent source of information, in that he falls on a different side of the argument compared to some of the other historians named above. Braham is extremely critical of Horthy and his administration, and lays a great deal of blame on Horthy for the fate of the Jews in Hungary, though he does not go quite as far in his critique and condemnation of Horthy as, for instance, the communists who labeled Horthy fascist. With Braham, however, it must be noted that the fact that he is Jewish, along with his own experiences in a Hungarian labor battalion during the war, likely have had some impact on how he treats the topic of the Horthy regime. Braham's book, along with other works written and edited by him, will serve as a source to compare to the other histories of Hungary between the wars and during World War II, and may serve as a challenge to some of the conclusions I have drawn from my own research.[10]

Perhaps more important, however, are the translated primary sources. While some of the major figures of the Horthy era, such as Prime Ministers Istvan Bethlen and Gyula Gombos, unfortunately never wrote any sort of memoir, others, including Horthy himself, Prime Minister Miklos Kallay, and Prime Minister Geza Lakatos wrote memoirs which have been translated into English. I make use largely of Horthy's memoir, the memoir of his daughter in law, Countess Ilona Edelsheim-Gyulai, and the account of John Flournoy Montgomery, the American minister to Hungary from 1933 to 1941. A different sort of primary source that I draw on frequently is a collection of translations of Horthy's papers. Other primary sources include

---

[10] Randolph L. *Braham, Politics of Genocide: The Holocaust in Hungary,* (Detroit, MI: Wayne State University Press, 2000).

memoirs of officials in Horthy's administration along with Jewish accounts from the period.

The memoir of Miklos Horthy is one of the most obvious primary sources to draw on for this analysis. First published in 1953, there are several editions, the latest released in 2000, which includes annotations by Andrew Simon, Professor Emeritus at the University of Akron, which add clarity to names and events Horthy mentions, along with some supplementary material in the appendices, including a transcript of the speech delivered by Horthy in 1944 when he attempted to take Hungary out of the war, as well as recollections and interviews with his daughter-in-law, Ilona Bowden. Of course, there are issues with bias and inconsistencies in the memoir, which Horthy wrote at an advanced age, from memory while in exile after the war. However, the memoir cannot simply be disregarded, and even taking into account inaccuracies, many things can be proven accurate through comparison to other sources, in addition to the insight it gives the reader into Horthy the man, looking back at his time in power.[11] The annotator, Andrew Simon, perhaps puts it best when he states that the volume is not meant to be simply a presentation of Horthy's memoirs, but a skeleton to tell the story of Hungary during the Horthy years.[12] Horthy's memoir cannot be the sole source used to understand his quarter century in office, but it serves as a starting point from which to branch out to other, more varied and perhaps more consistently reliable sources.

One such source, which proved invaluable for this analysis, is the memoir of Countess Ilona Edelsheim-Gyulai (later Ilona Bowden), Horthy's daughter in law, which was released only in the year 2000 (the English translation in 2005), and which devotes considerable space to the crucial period from 1940 through the end of the war.[13] The memoir's usefulness is unfortunately

---

[11] Miklos Horthy and Andrew L. Simon, *Admiral Nicholas Horthy: Memoirs* (Safety Harbor, FL: Simon Publications, 2000), 2.

[12] Simon, 2-3.

[13] She married Horthy's oldest son, Istvan, in 1940. Istvan died in 1942, but Ilona remained with the family and was intimately involved with the events preceding and during the German occupation of Hungary.

limited by the fact that Bowden only became a part of the Horthy family in 1940, but for those crucial, controversial years, her account provides a good deal of insight. Despite the fact that she wrote it many years later, much of the memoir, in particular the war years, was written with the aid of a diary she kept during that time, allowing her to more accurately recount what she felt and experienced decades earlier, when she was very directly involved in the political machinations of the time, including the period during the German occupation. Due to its recent release, almost none of the published secondary sources were able to draw on this primary source, and its inclusion here will hopefully allow this analysis to break new ground.[14]

John Flournoy Montgomery's *Hungary: The Unwilling Satellite*, is another primary account that provides an interesting perspective on much of the Horthy Era while posing similar problems as the memoirs.[15] Montgomery was the American minister to Hungary from 1933 to 1941, and had a front row seat during the tumultuous time when the country fell into Germany's orbit. This is his book's theme. His stated goal is to portray Hungary to Americans as largely a victim of German foreign policy conquests. Montgomery provides insight into both political developments as well as more personal moments he experienced with the Horthy family.[16] However, Montgomery's friendship with the Horthy family must be noted when considering his opinions on the Horthy administration (the book even contains a facsimile of a letter he sent to Horthy while he was being held by the Allies before the Nuremberg trials, where Horthy was not charged with any crimes.)[17] That said, the information

---

[14] Ilona Bowden, *Honour and Duty The Memoirs of Countess Ilona Edelsheim Gyulai Widow of Stephen Horthy, Vice-regent of Hungary* (Lewes, UK: Purple Pagoda Press Ltd, 200.

[15] John Flournoy Montgomery, *Hungary: The Unwilling Satellite* (Morristown, NJ: Vista Books, 1993).

[16] Montgomery, *ii*-12.

[17] After his deposition, Horthy was held by the Germans in Bavaria. At the war's end, he was first liberated, then arrested by the Unites States Army. He was not tried for war crimes; the only postwar leader who pushed for charges to be filed was Josip Broz Tito of Yugoslavia, but without the support of Stalin on the matter, nothing came of it and Horthy was released in 1945. In 1948 he provided

provided seems to be largely accurate, and historians have not been as critical of Montgomery's book as with Horthy's memoir. Montgomery's book fills a unique space, as it is among the only primary accounts (aside from Horthy's) written by someone with access to key figures during the 1930s and early 1940s. It will prove key to piecing together what transpired, as perceived by an outsider looking in.

The final key primary source that I will touch on here is the collection of Horthy's papers, compiled and translated into English in the volume *The Confidential Papers of Admiral Horthy*, by Miklos Szinai and Laszlo Szucs. The collection features dozens of papers, ranging from letters written to figures such as Adolf Hitler and Hungarian Prime Minister Bardossy, to letters written to Horthy by the notables surrounding him, to personal letters and transcripts.[18] Unfortunately, there is relatively little included in the volume (which does not claim to be a complete collection of Horthy's surviving papers) relating to the later years of the war, those documents having been lost or destroyed. There is, however, a great deal from the interwar period and early 1940s, all translated into English by Szinai and Szucs. Additionally, the book includes the original versions of most, if not all, of the papers, and even photographs of a select few. There are also notes along with the translations, which contextualize each document.[19]

However, something that has to be taken into account is that this book was originally published in Budapest in 1965, in the middle of Hungary's communist period. In some of the background paragraphs and other areas where the compilers write original text, some biases can be seen, though it is difficult to tell whether this was due to their own ideology or to a need to tread carefully when discussing Horthy during that time, but the compilers do seem to at least casually subscribe to the standard communist view of

---

testimony for the trial of Edmund Veesenmayer, who had been Germany's plenipotentiary in Hungary during the occupation.

[18] Miklos Szinai and Laszlo Szucs, *The Confidential Papers of Admiral Horthy* (Budapest: Corvina Press, 1965), *v-x*, 125, 183.

[19] Szinai and Szucs, *xxi-xxii*, 336.

Horthy.[20] Fortunately, any potential bias would for the most part only impact the selection of documents as well as the notes featured along with the documents, and the documents can be allowed to stand on their own as the only available primary sources that were written during the years this paper will analyze.

---

[20] Szinai and Szucs, *xii-xx*.

CHAPTER 1

Hungary In A New Age

Part 1: Prologue

The First World War came to an end on November 11, 1918. Hungary, which had been part of the Austro-Hungarian Empire, found itself on the losing side. The years 1918 and 1919 were tumultuous ones that would set Hungary on the course that would end with an alliance with Nazi Germany, then occupation by Nazi Germany, and then falling under communist domination. While the focus of this analysis will be on the Horthy era, which lasted from 1920 to 1944, it is impossible to properly understand what transpired in Hungary during that quarter century without first understanding the sequence of events that led to Horthy becoming regent.

Less than a month before the war's end, on October 16, 1918, Hungary's Prime Minister, Sandor Wekerle, declared an end to the union between Hungary and Austria, making Hungary an independent state for the first time in almost four hundred years. Despite public approbation of this news, Wekerle resigned shortly thereafter, and was replaced by Count Mihaly Karolyi on November 2. Two days after the official end of the war, on November 13, Emperor Charles IV surrendered the right to govern (without formally abdicating his position), and Hungary became a republic through an essentially bloodless revolution known as the Chrysanthemum Revolution.[21]

---

[21] See Hugh Seton-Watson, *Eastern Europe Between the Wars, 1918-1941* (Boulder: Westview Press, 1986), 185; Istvan Deak, *Hungary from 1918 to 1945* (New York: Columbia University, Institute on East Central Europe, 1986), 1; Maria Ormos,

Karolyi, despite being an aristocrat, held fairly liberal views, and worked closely with noted liberal sociologist Oszkar Jaszi. He became the face of the new Hungarian republic. The new government, made up of Hungary's moderate left, attempted to mend the growing rifts between the various nationalities that were a part of the not-yet divided Hungary, but while the Karolyi government initially enjoyed widespread support, this idealistic administration was quickly faced with the increasingly harsh reality of its situation. The government quickly did what it could to make itself look appealing to the victorious Entente, immediately announcing its intention to enter the soon-to-be formed League of Nations, and began withdrawing and then disbanding Hungary's armed forces. Additionally, Karolyi ended up highly dependent on socialist groups and trade unions. Unfortunately, the hoped for Entente support never materialized, while disbanding the army only encouraged Hungary's new neighbors to seize territory. The economy was also in dire straights, and more radical groups on both the left and the right began to agitate.[22]

Karolyi's republic lasted a mere six weeks. The moderately left-wing government, wishing to not limit free expression, was reluctant to take action to stifle radicals groups, which allowed the Hungarian communist movement to grow. Bela Kun and several other revolutionaries returned from the Soviet Union on November 17, where they had been closely involved with the recent communist revolution. Over the next several months, the Communists efficiently mobilized various groups, such as the unemployed, idle soldiers, and war wounded to demonstrate against the government, sometimes violently. This came to a head on February 20, 1919, when communists

---

"World War and Revolutions, 1914-1919. The New State Organization, 1920-1921," *Hungary: Governments and Politics 1848-2000*, ed. Maria Ormos and Bela K. Kiraly, translated by Nora Arato (Highland Lakes, NJ: Social Science Monographs, Boulder, CO: Atlantic Research and Publications, Inc, 2001), 179-181.
[22] Seton-Watson, 139-141; Ormos, 180-181; Deak, 14-15.

attacked the offices of a major Social Democratic[23] newspaper, killing several people in the process. Only at this point did the Karolyi government take action and arrest the communist leadership.[24]

By the beginning of 1919, the Karolyi government had begun to collapse as it became hopelessly caught in the middle of the strengthening political extremes while failing to shore up a party of the center. After the aforementioned arrest of the communist leaders (and a failed attempt to do the same to the far right leadership), the final blow came. On March 20, 1919, following decisions made at the Paris Peace Conference—to which no Hungarian representative had been invited—a memorandum was delivered to Karolyi by the senior representative of the Entente in Budapest, which simply informed Karolyi of the conference's decision. This memorandum stated that Hungary was to vacate an additional part of central Hungary and allow Romanian forces to move in. It was clear that this action was not to be a temporary one, and Karolyi rejected the demand, forcing him to abandon his previous policy of non-belligerence and Entente support. In a last-ditch effort to salvage the situation, he attempted to call for assistance from the Soviet Union with the aid of the Social Democrats. However, the Social Democrats moved first, meeting with the still imprisoned communist leadership, and came to a power sharing agreement. By March 22, Karolyi and many ministers resigned, and, as C. A. Macartney puts it, the red regime of Bela Kun replaced the pink regime of Karolyi. The Hungarian Soviet Republic was born.[25]

While it would not last long, Bela Kun's Soviet Republic would arguably have as much impact on the development of Hungary during the Horthy era as did the collapse of the Austro-Hungarian Empire and the subsequent Treaty of Trianon. While the communist regime that swept into power did

---

[23] Hungary's Social Democratic Party, which existed before the war, was ostensibly Marxist but in practice were more of a moderate left, promoting liberal causes such as universal suffrage, a shorter workday, and welfare programs.

[24] Deak, 13-15.

[25] Ignac Romsics, *Hungary in the Twentieth Century*, (Budapest: Corvina Books Ltd, Osiris, 1999), 98-99; C. A. Macartney, *Hungary: A Short History*, (Edinburgh: The Edinburgh University Press, 1962), 205.

enjoy support early on (as had the Karolyi government) the way in which it attained control, essentially via a putsch, differed wildly from the mass demonstrations and gradually growing desire for change that had ushered in the republic. There was next to no warning of the communist takeover, and the average Hungarian was caught completely by surprise when, on March 22, red flags flew throughout Budapest.[26]

While ideologically Bela Kun and his associates were true communists in the spirit of Lenin and believed in the primacy of class conflict over and above national loyalty, Kun was at the same time a Hungarian patriot, and the prevailing desire in Hungary was to reclaim the territories occupied by the successor states, as it was clear that those states were not going to be compelled to return the territory by the Entente. As a result, plans began for an offensive aimed to reclaim the lost territory. Despite the army being in shambles—by mid-April the army had barely over 60,000 men—and despite the neighboring Romanian and French forces being categorically superior, the Hungarians managed surprising success against the weaker Czechoslovakia, conquering most of Slovakia by early June, and the advance was stopped only by an ultimatum from Entente representative Georges Clemenceau. This was followed by a demand on June 13 that ordered Hungary to withdraw from the captured territory. Kun complied completely, both because Hungary had no chance of holding its own against the Entente powers should they intervene, and in order to defend his regime against the growing counter-revolutionary movement in Hungary. Indeed, this was the point at which the communist regime began its rapid decline.[27]

The effect that Bela Kun's regime had on antisemitism in Hungary likewise deserves attention. Of course, antisemitism was nothing new to Hungary. Even before the collapse of Austria-Hungary and the end of the war, Christian nationalism had been a growing force in Hungary, a reaction against "progressive" politics, which was heavily connected to the Jews, due to their prevalence in the leadership of left-leaning groups. There was a fear among many Christian Hungarians of "Jewish values" taking over society, in

---

[26] Romsics, 101.
[27] Romsics, 105-107; Seton-Watson, 147-149.

addition to the older religious concerns about Jews. However, under Habsburg rule, the ruling elites openly opposed antisemitic rhetoric as something that harmed national unity, and encouraged Jewish assimilation.[28]

As the war effort began to collapse and Austria-Hungary started to fracture, however, these thoughts and concerns were no longer held back, and those adhering to the emerging idea of Christian Hungary acutely felt the perceived threat of the Jews, particularly the Jews' responsibility for unwanted social and cultural change. Even higher ranking Church officials, such the Catholic bishop of Szekesfehervar, Ottokar Prohaszka, openly voiced their dread of "Jewish influence." He also believed that Hungary's Jews were avoiding military service. He maintained that on the front line one found true Christian Hungarians, putting their life on the line for their country, while the Jews would be found in safer positions behind the lines. He argued that "Jewish shirkers" would be the ones to shape the postwar culture and society in Hungary. At the same time, however, he denied being antisemitic. Rather, he argued that he was acting in "national self-defense." Unsurprisingly, Jewish public figures spoke out to refute such claims with reliable data. Even the prominent former prime minister, Istvan Tisza, spoke against the antisemitic accusations. The Right continued to see the Jews as threat to every aspect of the nation, thereby staking out a position distinct from that of the old elites, who may have wished to limit "Jewish influence," but did not view Hungary's Jews as such a threat.[29]

During the time of the Karolyi government, the Right, which had already been wary of his left-leaning policies, broke even further with the liberal Karolyi after his administration first failed in petitioning the Entente to restore lost Hungarian territory, and then did not use military force to defend the nation. The Right began relying on a heavily Christian-national message, and in late 1918 significant counterrevolutionary organizations formed, including the Association of Awakening Magyars (EME) and the Hungarian National Defense Association (MOVE). These groups were largely made up

---

[28] Paul A. Hanebrink, *In Defense of Christian Hungary: Religion, Nationalism, and Antisemitism, 1890-1944* (Ithaca, NY: Cornell University Press, 2006), 43-46.
[29] Hanebrink, 55-59.

of former military officers and politicians. Adding further fuel to the antisemitic rhetoric and the Right's growing fear of Jews trying to transform Hungary into something alien was the fact that the majority of high ranking officials in Bela Kun's communist regime were of Jewish origin. If anything confirmed their fears, this was it, regardless of the fact that the majority of Jews in Hungary were just as opposed to the communist government.[30]

Along with the seizure of power by the communists came what has come to be known as the "Red Terror," a common feature of communist revolutions. The Hungarian Red Terror took place primarily after the regime's military failure, in response to its rapidly waning popularity. Following communist dogma, the government nationalized large estates as well as many businesses, which led to a sharp decline in production, and farmers refused to accept the new currency, which meant that food stopped reaching the cities. The regime responded with forced requisitions, which led to increased peasant resistance. Harsh punishments were meted out under the leadership of Tibor Szamuely and Jozsef Cserny's "Lenin Boys," the most infamous of the communist paramilitary groups. However, these measures ultimately failed as the counterrevolution gained steam, and segments of the military began to mutiny. On August 1, the Revolutionary Governing Council resigned and fled abroad—a mere 133 days after they had come into power. Szamuely escaped as well, though Cserny was later captured and executed during the White Terror that accompanied the counter-revolutionaries.[31]

Counterrevolutionary groups began forming almost immediately after the communists took power, emerging in Vienna as well as in two cities in Hungary under French control, Szeged and Arad. Meanwhile, in Budapest, the Hungarian Soviet Republic was still in place, at least officially, headed for six days by Gyula Peidl, during which time he undertook the task of undoing the many unpopular policies and actions of his predecessors, before the counterrevolutionary forces took control on August 6.[32]

---

[30] Hanebrink, 66-70; Romsics, 99-100; Deak, 15.
[31] Deak, 16-17; Seton-Watson, 188; Romsics, 100-101.
[32] Romsics, 108.

As previously mentioned, however, the counterrevolution had been developing since at least the spring of 1919, and the leadership of the groups featured a number of important figures who would play significant roles during the coming decades. Istvan Bethlen (who led the group in Vienna), Gyula Karolyi (who headed the Szeged government), and Gyula Gombos, would all later serve as prime minister. By the end of May, the counterrevolutionary movement largely solidified and merged in Szeged, and invited Vice-Admiral Miklos Horthy to serve as minister of defense, in command of the counterrevolutionary national army they were building. Horthy brought several things to the table which contributed to his selection by the counterrevolutionaries. In addition to having been a career naval officer, during which time he had risen to become the commander in chief of Austria-Hungary's Adriatic fleet, he had achieved somewhat of a hero status during the war with his victory at the Battle of the Strait of Otranto.[33] Horthy had also served as an aide-de-camp to the late Emperor Franz Josef, which gave the counterrevolutionary movement a connection to the monarchy.[34]

The building of what came to be called the National Army was facilitated by the occupying French, who had no love for the communist regime. They allowed soldiers into Szeged, though they did place restrictions on weapons. The army eventually grew to nearly 30,000 strong, but it never fought a real battle. When Bela Kun and his top associates fled the country, only a tiny fraction of the army was headed toward Budapest, and its movements were subject to direction by both the French and Romanian occupying forces in Hungary. It was not until November 16 that the army reached Budapest, after the Romanians had pulled out, and Horthy triumphantly entered the city riding a white horse. However, the counterrevolution is remembered

---

[33] On May 14, 1917, the then Captain Miklos Horthy led a raid on the Allied blockade at the Strait of Otranto. It was the only significant Austro-Hungarian naval victory of the war, and Horthy gained additional renown for the fact that after being wounded in battle he continued to command until he lost consciousness. Ultimately, it had little impact on the war, but with so little success overall, both the battle and its commander were well known and highly regarded.

[34] Romsics, 107-109; Deak, 17; Ormos, 197-198.

primarily for the White Terror that came along with it, a spree of targeted attacks and lynchings of people associated with the deposed regime. This included those who had held administrative positions in Bela Kun's regime, those who had served in the Red Army, and Jews—many, if not most, of whom had no connection to the communist regime. The White Terror, by all accounts, surpassed the Red Terror in scale and brutality, as commando units affiliated with Horthy's army but acting unrepentantly—carried out this "revenge." The White Terror mostly subsided by the end of 1919, but attacks associated with it continued into 1920, until Horthy—who had not given orders to carry out the terror, but at the same time had been aware and had given his tacit approval—had the violence stopped, and order restored.[35]

After the success of the counterrevolution, things moved quickly. After ousting the remaining communists, a counterrevolutionary government was established in Budapest on August 6 (well before Horthy and the army arrived.) Soon after, the government at Szeged formally dissolved itself and its ministers took positions in the Friedrich government. Horthy, who had been commander in chief of the army in Szeged, now became so in Budapest. When the Habsburg Archduke Joseph, who the new government had wanted to become its head, was forced to withdraw at the demand of the Allied Powers, things were reshuffled yet again and a new government was formed. On December 1, Hungary was at last invited to send a delegation to Paris to receive the peace terms, and they were announced on January 15, 1920. Shortly thereafter the first election of a National Assembly, a parliament that had been originally conceived by Mihaly Karolyi, was held. Most citizens were eligible to vote, but it took place as the White Terror was still going on, which certainly had an impact on the results. The resulting government was profoundly reactionary, and Christian in character—as opposed to Jewish, which still implied communism—and completely without any communist or socialist

---

[35] Ormos, 202-205; Deak, 17; Sakmyster, 30-32; Bela Bodo, "Paramilitary Violence in Hungary After the First World War," *Eastern European Quarterly* 38, no. 2 (2004): 4-9.

representation; the former was banned, and the latter abstained from voting.[36]

As the Allies would not accept a government headed by a Habsburg, by February the decision was made to elect a regent, which would allow Hungary to nominally remain a kingdom and potentially leave the option open for change in the future while complying with the terms of the Paris Peace Conference. On March 1, Horthy was elected regent by an overwhelming majority of 131 out of 141 delegates in the National Assembly, and the Horthy era formally began.[37]

Understanding the effect of this not quite two year long period will allow us to understand both why important individuals and Hungary as a whole moved in the directions they did over the next two decades. In particular, the impact of Bela Kun's short-lived communist regime cannot be underestimated. This impact can be clearly seen in Horthy's memoir. After Hungary gave up its navy as part of the post-war requirements, Horthy writes that he believed his military career was at an end, and he returned to his family estate at Kenderes. For several months he remained there, uninvolved with public affairs, though he was aware of the political developments, referring to the Karolyi government disparagingly as "defeatists" in his memoir, and he notes with sadness that the October 31, 1918, murder of Count Istvan Tisza, a mentor of his and a well known symbol of the old order, as a symbol of defeat.[38]

As distasteful as Horthy found Hungary after the Karolyi revolution— Sakmyster describes him as having been so strongly devoted to the old order that he could not appreciate even the good intentions of the new system— Horthy seemed relatively content to return to civilian life, overseeing his estate, and was not particularly interested in any sort of counterrevolution— not yet, at least. Sakmyster relates one incident in early 1919 when Horthy

---

[36] Joseph Rothschild, *East Central Europe between the Two World Wars* (Seattle: University of Washington Press, 1977), 152-154; Romsics, 112-114.

[37] Rothschild, 154; Romsics, 114-115; Ormos, 205-207.

[38] Miklos Horthy and Andrew L. Simon, *Admiral Nicholas Horthy: Memoirs* (Safety Harbor, FL: Simon Publications, 2000), 110-111; Sakmyster, 12-14.

happened to travel to Budapest and met with several military officers, including Gyula Gombos, who were already a vocal opposition to the new government, having formed the Association of Hungarian National Defense (MOVE). Gombos made mention of organizational issues they were having, and tried to convince Horthy to assume the position of leader of the movement. Horthy refused to do so. He saw MOVE's plans as bold, but highly impractical, and did not feel that any action could be taken to change the situation for quite some time.[39]

One could certainly speculate on whether or not Horthy would ever have gotten involved in opposition politics should the Karolyi government have managed to stay in power, but its collapse and the rise of Bela Kun's Bolshevik regime certainly had a great impact on him. In his memoir, Horthy's first descriptors used to characterize the regime are "bloodthirsty," and "horror." And perhaps more significantly for Horthy personally, the violence and unrest even reached his hometown of Kenderes. Horthy describes some of the reprisals meted out in response to the peasant rebellions. While the local peasants apparently did not harass the wealthy landowners as the revolutionary forces urged them to, it is very possible that either Horthy or one of his close family members had an unpleasant interaction with revolutionaries which made his hatred of communism more personal. But no specific incident is described in his memoir. Regardless, it is clear that as he remained on his estate, Horthy was keeping track of current events, and growing increasingly concerned. Despite this, he did not seek out a role in the counterrevolution; only when he was petitioned by first Count Gyula Karolyi and then by Count Istvan Bethlen, who held similar political views to Horthy's, requesting him to take up the position as commander and organizer of a national army, did he depart Kenderes and make the dangerous journey to Szeged a few weeks later.[40] Here, as he took his first step back into active public life, we see the beginning of a pattern that would by and large hold

---

[39] Horthy, 112-113, 117-118; Sakmyster, 13-15.
[40] Kenderes was in between the two dangerous areas controlled by the communists and occupying Romanians, respectively, neither of which would take kindly to his attempt to travel to French-held Szeged and raise an army.

true throughout his eventual quarter-century in office; despite being a man of strong convictions, Horthy tended to rely on the advice of those he trusted rather than acting on his own. In this case, he knew and trusted both Karolyi and Bethlen. As we will see, this characteristic would at times work out very well, but other times it led to poor decisions.

Before we continue, we must introduce the important issue of the Jews, specifically in regard to Horthy himself. While Horthy's feelings toward Hungary's Jews is a critical issue, a starting point must be established. There is no concrete information on his views prior to the First World War, but based on the circles he frequented, it is fair to suggest that he simultaneously held some form of antisemitic ideas, as was common among the Austro-Hungarian military's officers, as well as idolizing and seeking to emulate Emperor Franz Joseph, who was known to hold tolerant views regarding the Jews. Under Franz Joseph's rule, Austro-Hungarian Jews had full civil liberties and many career opportunities, and a number had been granted titles for their civil service. Of course, most Jews in the latter category, as well as most Jews Horthy might have met, would have been assimilated Jews.[41]

However, during the period of the Karolyi government, Horthy, like many aristocrats and former officers, saw Hungary as becoming too heavily influenced by "Jewish values," and at one instance referred to Karolyi as a "Jewish stooge" in facilitating the later communist revolution. Regarding the Bolsheviks, Horthy mentions that the Kun regime was almost completely run by Jews, but states that the local Jews quickly denounced the regime. It is possible, however—if not likely—that this assertion is among the inaccuracies in the memoir, as even Sakmyster writes that Horthy, on some level, believed that "the Jews" were responsible for the war and revolutions. Despite what he writes in the memoir, it is highly likely that Horthy did, at the time, at least hold Jews as a group broadly responsible for at least the communist revolution.[42]

Also setting the tone for the interwar period was Horthy's distaste for Hungary's neighbors, often referred to as the "Successor States:"

---

[41] Sakmyster, 7.
[42] Sakmyster, 12, 17; Horthy, 114.

Czechoslovakia, Romania, and Yugoslavia. They were enemies as much as the communists, and he paints them as rampaging aggressors. His family personally suffered monetary loss due to the continued Romanian advance in particular. Additionally, he attributes the few successes of Bela Kun's Red Army to officers not loyal to him, but to the Hungarian nation. Upon assuming command of the fledgling national army, he launched into the task of its growth. He details his dealings with the Romanian government as well as with the French while he gathered forces, and was able to come to an agreement with the Romanians quickly, while the French, who were wary of a return of the Habsburgs, were more difficult. He clearly saw himself as a defender of historic Hungary, and sought to "cleanse" it of communism. However, he remained cautious, and did not march to Budapest even once he received news of Kun's flight and the initial counterrevolutionary coup headed in Budapest itself. His presence greatly improved the morale of those in Szeged due to his wartime reputation, and despite his new army never fighting any true battles, his popularity surged among both the military and civilian sectors; he was a symbol of both present authority and the old order, and began to establish a rapport with western officials.[43]

The counterrevolutionary government at Szeged was made up of officials spanning the spectrum from liberal to conservative to far-right; however, the officer corps leaned far more to the right, and it was among them that Horthy, as a military man, spent a great deal of time and proved sympathetic to their more radical idea. When these influences were compounded with the knowledge that his family's property had been looted by both the Romanians and communists, and the fact that his eldest daughter had died of illness not long before, it is hardly surprising that he was in an angry, vengeful frame of mind by the time he entered Budapest on his famous white horse on November 16.[44]

It was almost immediately after this that the White Terror began in earnest. While there is no evidence of Horthy ever giving an order to carry out revenge attacks, it is highly unlikely that he was unaware, which leaves

---

[43] Horthy, 115-123; Sakmyster, 18-23.
[44] Horthy, 123-124; Sakmyster, 22-25.

Horthy in the position of tacitly approving, or at least knowing but ignoring. He was also slow to react when liberal elements of the counterrevolution spoke out against the atrocities. Pronay, the most infamous of the revenge detachment leaders, would even become Horthy's bodyguard for a time. In his memoir, he does not outright condemn the White Terror, mentioning it only in passing and just briefly referring to injustices and atrocities. In fact, he provides some justification for the vengeful feelings, and though he maintains that he and his headquarters never issued a "bloodthirsty order," he intimates that at least some form of reprisal was warranted. As Sakmyster writes, this attitude demonstrates both his profound fear and hatred of communism and also the influence of the Gomboses and Pronays around him.[45]

His tone softened some time after, when he was approached by a group of conservative aristocratic officials including Bethlen, who emphasized that the reprisals would only hurt Hungary in the greater scheme of things and that it eroded the army's honor. While he initially rebuffed their suggestions, he apparently did take their words to heart, and he returned to a more conservative mindset, and gradually took steps to lessen the impact of the White Terror. He would grant exemptions to some of the accused citizens, and took care not to instigate violence against Jews in his speeches. When he finally spoke to Pronay in particular about toning things down, Pronay was surprised at the change, but Horthy did not reverse his opinion again. He took steps to present a better image of himself and the counterrevolution he represented, and met with more liberal Hungarian factions as well as with British representatives. Before entering Budapest, he agreed to make the army subservient to the new government as well as to obligate it to respect civil rights even as it "fought Bolshevism." These developments also increased Horthy's standing with foreign officials, who, sharing his anti-communist views, heaped praise on him. When the army entered Budapest, there was no pogrom, as some had feared. In fact, it is argued by some that the excesses of the White Terror, the almost uncontrollable rage of the far right, is what first

---

[45] Horthy, 124-126; Sakmyster, 23-25; Seton-Watson, 189; Bodo, 9-19.

set the modern far right at odds with Hungary's conservative right, which Horthy would come to identify with. However, there should be no illusion that this discomfort was due to the treatment of Jews and leftists by the paramilitary groups. Rather, it was due to a desire by the elite to maintain a sense of order and control. The militia groups were seen as too wild. While the far right wished to transform Hungary into something "greater," the aristocratic elite wished to maintain as much of the pre-war status quo as possible. And, as mentioned before, the far right, unlike the conservatives elites, sought to place value on people based on their race or religion, rather than a more pragmatic view of who provides the most benefit to society. The break between Horthy and Pronay is emblematic of the divide between the two groups, who had joined forces in response to the communist regime.[46]

Soon a new, temporary coalition government under Prime Minister Karoly Huszar was established. As elections were prepared, Horthy vacillated between the conservative advice of Bethlen and that of Gombos, who sought to push Horthy toward a military dictatorship by way of his election as regent. While Horthy later asserted that he had never sought a leadership position, he did campaign for election, prompted by Gombos. Horthy does not personally discuss much of what led up to his election as regent, though he does describe an alleged assassination attempt on him, which led to a "regrettable" outbreak of violence directed at communists and Jews. Horthy, in his writings, sounds surprised that he had been elected regent, but it can hardly have been so surprising. He was certainly aware that he was considered a viable candidate, and that his army was conspicuously present during the vote. Horthy would ultimately accept this appointment, but with certain conditions that will be discussed below.[47]

As important as Horthy was at this time, and the significance of the events surrounding him, it must be remembered that in the end he was still just one man, with a limited ability to influence larger societal trends. Additionally, it

---

[46] Horthy, 126-128; Sakmyster, 39-46; Bodo, 30-33; Bela Bodo, "Hungarian Aristocracy and the White Terror," *Journal of Contemporary History,* 45, no. 4 (2010): 720-724.

[47] Horthy, 128-131; Sakmyster, 48-57.

is important to note that while we have been primarily focusing on the more right-leaning segments of Hungarian society, in these early years there was a greater variety of viewpoints. One such viewpoint was that of Oszkar Jaszi, who was a left-leaning social scientist who served a minister in the Mihaly Karolyi government. From his writings, it is clear that his goal was a democratic system in Hungary; he viewed the old regime as outdated and militaristic. From the outset, he acknowledged lack of organization as a crucial problem for both the revolution and organizing the new government. Nonetheless, he describes the revolution as having broad support and himself as greatly optimistic at the initial success of the revolution. His excitement leaps out of the pages of his writing while discussing its success.[48]

The key goals of the new administration, as laid out by him, included Hungary becoming completely independent, dealing with minority nationalities in the "Wilsonian" way, and democratizing the government. However, it quickly became apparent to him that the elements necessary to keep the new system afloat were lacking. [49] Reading his account, one gets the impression that he saw earlier than most that the new system was already in decline, and that his plan for keeping Hungary intact by convincing minority leaders to keep their populations within the borders of Hungary in exchange for full autonomy, was not working either. He resigned his government position in the hope that from outside the government he could better promote his views.[50]

Shortly after the communist takeover on March 21, 1919, Jaszi left the country. He writes that he could not tolerate the new regime's denial of freedom of thought. He also adds that he predicted in advance that the communist government would soon collapse in the face of a counterrevolution. Jaszi, who was himself an assimilated Jew, also addressed the fact that such a high percentage of the communist leadership was Jewish. In his view, communists favor strict rationalism over morality, which he

---

[48] Oszkar Jaszi, *Revolution and Counter-Revolution in Hungary* (New York: H. Fertig, 1969), 28-35.
[49] Jaszi, 38
[50] Jaszi, 75-77, 86.

attributes to some Jews as well, as finds another parallel comparing the almost messianic message of communism with the messianic beliefs of some Jews. He also notes the fact that communism was the first political system in centuries in which Jews could participate. However, his explanation of the theory of communism as a purely Jewish creation is pointedly inaccurate.[51]

While he and Horthy shared a distaste for communism, however, Jaszi had just as strong a dislike for the counterrevolution, and refers to Horthy and his associates as terrorists. He strongly decries the antisemitic characteristic of the counterrevolution, and labels the White Terror one of the darkest moments in Hungary's history. As the Horthy regime took shape, Jaszi continued to attack it—from abroad.[52]

Significant movements like Hungary's communist movement and the Christian nationalist movement do not appear overnight, however, and as strong personalities as both Horthy and Jaszi were, they were limited in power just like any other individuals in Hungarian society. To gain an understanding of some of the underlying causes of these calamitous revolutions, Paul Hanebrink's *In Defense of Christian Hungary* in especially useful. Prior to the First World War, he explains, there was extreme cultural anxiety in Hungary, specifically about whether the greatest threat to Hungary's national sovereignty was internal or external. Both major Christian sects in Hungary—Catholics and largely Calvinist Protestants—inflamed worries of "alien" cultural ideas undermining Hungary's social order and leading to increasing secularism and moral decay. Their solutions, by and large, consisted of strongly reasserting religion in daily life, that is defending "Christian" Hungary. Unsurprisingly, these discussions of Hungary as a Christian nation raised the ever-present Jewish question to the forefront, and as a result some of the old religious based anti-Jewish lines of thought merged with new concerns over "Jewish values" having too much influence in society. While this idea of a Christian Hungary existed before the war, it gained little traction as the aristocratic elites were opposed to any sort of rhetoric that would bring about disunity. By the war's end, however, the old order was

---

[51] Jaszi, 110-111, 122-124.
[52] Jaszi, 154-160.

collapsing, and this attitude began to spread. The fact that most Jews had not supported the communist regime, and that most (if not all) of those involved in the Kun regime did not identify as Jews, did not matter.[53]

Near the end of the war, Hungary's liberal left began to assert itself, with figures such as Mihaly Karolyi and Oszkar Jaszi coming to the forefront. They and other progressive democrats sought to reshape Hungary into a more democratic state. Some in their circle, however, took a more radical point of view and argued that religion had no place in a modern, progressive society if it could not be reconciled with secular ideals. When the chance to put a new system in place came in 1918, however, it came as a surprise, and the governing coalition ended up being very mixed. Despite the fact that the left had not actually changed much, the Hungarian right, sometimes termed the "new Right," found the left's ideas extremely threatening. Quickly, some prominent figures on the right made statements equating any sort of change with Bolshevism, and Hanebrink writes that many in Hungary at this point started to see the culture war they had feared beginning at home, between "Christian Hungary" and the "other Hungary." In the final months of the war, these feelings were manifested in propaganda decrying a perceived lack of national faith on the home front. Christian leaders attacked "anti-Christian" groups including Jews, freemasons, and atheists. In one direct example of efforts to combat the "Jewish media," the Jesuit Father Bangha tried to raise money for a Christian press to counter the "other" influence.[54]

While Karolyi's government started off strong, it was clear from the outset that it was going to change significant parts of the social order. But it was the suggestion to completely separate church and state—removing religion from the public school system in particular—that worried both Catholic and Protestant leaders. When Karolyi's government failed to defend Hungary's borders, this religious concern merged with the fear of the collapse of the nation. This gave rise to a new idea of national history—the rebirth of the nation from the ashes of defeat. Drawing on classical Christian themes, the

---

[53] Hanebrink, 45-46; Ezra Mendelsohn, *The Jews of East Central Europe Between the World Wars* (Bloomington: Indiana University Press, 1983), 94-98.
[54] Hanebrink, 52-56.

right felt that the necessary rebirth would require a complete break with the liberal past, citing the recent national disaster and the perceived moral decay. Again, Jews were associated with the "other Hungary." When the republic collapsed and Bela Kun's communist regime took power, more fuel was added to the fire.[55]

Even more so than the republic, the communist regime was associated with Jews, quickly leading to the formation of counterrevolutionary movements, with the far right at its core. And as the secular nationalists prepared to form an army that would seek retribution, the religious nationalists came to share similar rhetoric, labeling Judeo-Bolshevism as the enemy, something easily expanded to all Jews. This rhetoric was, of course, followed by the White Terror, and as we will see throughout this analysis, the drive to redeem and purify "Christian Hungary" was to remain a driving force until the end of World War II.[56]

Understanding where a moment or an individual came from is key to understanding the movement or person itself. As we move forward into the Horthy era itself, it is crucial that we understand the impact the revolutions of 1918 and 1919—specifically the communist revolution—had not just on the major players, but on society as a whole. Between these events and the harsh terms of the 1921 Treaty of Trianon, Hungary's populace was set on a rightward course that no government or political figure could outright change, only manage, while Horthy and the Hungarian elite were attempting to maintain the old order.

Part 2: Horthy Ascendant

Horthy's appointment to the position of regent, and the specifics of what that position entailed, is crucial to understanding both what exactly his position meant and to the greater theme of consolidation and reorganization of Hungary in the 1920s. Hungary was nominally still a monarchy during this

---

[55] Hanebrink, 64-71.
[56] Hanebrink, 92-93, 106-107.

period, albeit with a regent instead of a king. As this was a relatively rare state of affairs, after Horthy's election via secret ballot the exact powers of the regent had to be demarcated. Initially, the regent was to have powers comparable to both that of a king in a system where a parliament makes the law or to the president of a republic. The regent—which, at the time it was created, was envisioned a temporary position, not one which would last a quarter century—importantly could not create a dynasty or create new nobles. The regent would represent the country in foreign relations and have the authority to sign treaties and appoint diplomats. The regent would also be sent new laws before they were approved by the parliament, and could send them back for reconsideration once; if passed again, they became law. The regent would also have the right to appoint prime ministers and could dissolve the Assembly—but only if it had been inactive or deadlocked for a significant period of time. Finally, the regent would also hold the title of Supreme War Lord and have sweeping power over military matters, but would not have the power to set its budget or declare war, and could not grant pardons. All in all, the office of the regent was designed as that of a standard head of state, limited enough that a military dictatorship did not arise, with some trappings of a monarch as evidenced by some of its powers and the title, Serene Highness.[57]

After the vote, however, Horthy initially declined to accept the position offered, arguing that the restrictions imposed on the regent would relegate him to a mere figurehead, without any ability to truly govern. His chief demands were greater discretion when it came to dismissing parliament and the ability to approve legislation. He also chafed at his inability to honor people with titles. These demands were relayed to parliament, and debate quickly ensued. Some felt Horthy was trying to position himself as a pseudo-monarch, while others thought he had a scheme in mind to reinstate Charles IV, the Hapsburg heir, to the position of king. At the same time, however, there was genuine fear of a military coup if these demands were denied. A compromise was reached, and Horthy was promised that the legislature would find a solution to adequately address his concerns. Horthy then traveled to

---

[57] Deak, 18-19; Romsics, 114-115; Sakmyster, 54-56.

the parliament building, where more detailed negotiations were held, and once he was satisfied with the promises he received, he promptly swore the oath and accepted the position as Regent of Hungary.[58]

What drove Horthy to accept the role, and why did he insist on additional powers before accepting at all? The easy answer, at first glance, might be that he simply was ambitious and knowing the power he already commanded via the military, pushed for more executive powers with full knowledge that his demands would be met. While it is certainly likely that Horthy had some ambition (and some of his associates certainly did on his behalf), the available evidence does not show Horthy as someone with a particular desire for power. It is important to note that he only became the leader of the counterrevolutionary army after being invited to do so, and while he did campaign for his election as regent, it was at the prompting of Gyula Gombos. Furthermore, Horthy refrained from taking full advantage of the powers bestowed upon him, and for a significant portion of his reign he was content to leave the day-to-day affairs of state to his prime minister and legislature.[59]

In his memoir, Horthy emphatically states that he did not seek to lead, rather that as an Hapsburg heir taking a position of leadership would not be tolerated by the rest of Europe, his nomination for consideration as regent was suggested without consulting him. He even names Count Albert Apponyi as the person he was personally hoping would be chosen. He then couches his initial reluctance to accept the position in his loyalty to the Hapsburgs; he had sworn an oath of loyalty to the royal line, and if he became regent he would have to swear a new oath to the nation and constitution, which could lead to a conflict of loyalties. He then states that the Assembly implored him to accept, and it eventually just asked for his demands, and suggested that he be granted essentially the powers of a king aside from the ability to create nobles and Church patronage. He then accepted out of a sense of duty and because he could think of no further reason to object. This of course does not completely match up with historical accounts, at least in the sense of Horthy's duty-oriented disposition.[60]

---

[58] Sakmyster, 55-57; Deak, 18-19; Romsics, 114-115; Szinai and Szucs, 9-10.
[59] Deak, 19.
[60] Horthy, 130-131.

He also makes no mention of the fact of his soldiers being conspicuously present on the day of the vote. This, therefore, begs the question of whether this omission is a product of writing decades later without any past papers, or something done deliberately to improve his image. Both are possible, but, as we will see further on, Horthy was not a particularly politically savvy person, and it is unlikely that he would deliberately alter events in his memoir. Most likely, regarding this instance at least, he remembered events in a more idealized way.

Something else worth remarking on regarding this series of events is Sakmyster's note that Horthy was accompanied by the now infamous Pal Pronay,[61] who commanded his bodyguard, when he traveled to discuss his appointment to the office of regent. Between the presence of Pronay, a member of the far right, and having been previously encouraged by Gyula Gombos to work toward becoming regent, it can also be argued that Horthy only became regent because these people he trusted pushed him to do so in the hope that he would further their radical agendas. This possibility is strengthened by an anecdote cited by Sakmyster, in which he describes Horthy making a spontaneous speech to his officers shortly after becoming regent. Afterward, it was Pronay who was disappointed in what he thought was a speech that "lacked logical content of a progression of ideas." Pronay began to doubt that Horthy would continue to do what he and others in the Szeged group had hoped for. It is certainly interesting that Pronay has misgivings when Horthy acted spontaneously. As we will see, Horthy indeed drifted away from the more radical ideas that had been prevalent in Szeged and by 1921 cut personal ties with Pronay.[62]

Horthy's rise to regent caused some in Hungary to worry, but by and large his appointment was welcome, and there was hope that now that the government was re-established and organized, things would calm down and life could progress as normal. Not long after, however, Hungary was forced to accept the infamous Treaty of Trianon, which would, more than anything

---

[61] Pronay remained on good terms with Horthy at this time, though soon after Pronay was reigned in and the White Terror ended they had a falling out.
[62] Sakmyster, 56-57; Bodo, 32.

else that happened in this postwar period, set Hungary's course going forward.

On June 4, 1920, a Hungarian delegation was summoned to Versailles where it was made to accept and sign the treaty. Dictates of the treaty included Hungary accepting responsibility for the start of the war, drastically shrinking its military, and ceding more than two thirds of its former territory. The territorial loss itself had further impact on Hungary, as it lost much of its prewar population (though it was now almost completely populated by ethnic Magyars), access to the sea, as well as significant amounts of its natural resources. And while Hungary was not the only country to face severe penalties in the postwar treaties, it was arguably hit the hardest.[63]

It is therefore hardly a surprise that anger over the terms of the treaty became both a driving and, at least for a time, a uniting force in Hungary. As we have previously seen, even when Hungary was under communist rule and territory was only occupied and not yet officially lost, there was such a desire for reclamation that the communist government attempted to take territory back by force. Everyone in Hungary at least paid lip service to the desire to see some form of territorial revision, to reclaim what was lost, and the slogan *"Nem, nem, soha!"* [No, no, never!] became the rallying cry of the new Hungary. Of course, this central goal was also easily used for political purposes. The national struggle could be used to justify almost any policy, and it would be very easy to label any political dissent as disloyalty to country and cause.[64]

In his memoir, Horthy devotes a significant amount of space detailing not just what the treaty entailed for Hungary, but the cynical nature of the treaty and the forces behind it, as he saw it. Horthy lays much of the blame on two of the successor states, Romania and Czechoslovakia, alleging secret treaties that had determined Hungary's fate before the war's end. He also points out that the treaty did not even allow for people in various regions to decide for themselves whether they would have preferred to remain part of Hungary. He concludes that section of his book on a more forward thinking note, stating that the "fragment of Hungary" still had to live and revitalize itself despite the

---

[63] Deak, 19-20.
[64] Deak, 19-20.

damage done to it. However, as we will see, Horthy never forgot about the injustices of Trianon, and thoughts of revision were always on his mind.[65]

Part 3: The Early Years

The first prime minister appointed by Horthy was Sandor Simonyi-Semadam, a lawyer who was a little known political figure. Simonyi-Semadam was not an obvious choice, and not Horthy's first choice; that would have been Istvan Bethlen, who belonged firmly to the conservative right and was despised by members of the far right like Pronay, who particularly took issue with Bethlen's more moderate attitude toward Hungary's Jews. In early 1920, however, Bethlen did not feel that the time was ripe for the programs he had in mind for Hungary—and both he and Horthy were well aware that Hungary was going to be made to sign the peace treaty soon, and whatever administration did so would by association become weakened. In essence, Simonyi-Semadam served as an interim prime minster, serving for just over four months until he and his government, having suffered the disgrace of signing the Treaty of Trianon as well as failing to prevent a boycott of Hungary by the International Federation of Trade Unions resigned.[66]

Horthy then selected Pal Teleki, another conservative—one who had been quite vocal against the violence of the White Terror—to the position of prime minister. Now that the treaty had been signed and its terms known, Hungary had to stabilize itself and move forward. Teleki began this process by putting an end to the final elements of the White Terror; he outlawed some of the activities of the far-right groups such as the Association of Awakening Magyars (EME), and corralled the military detachments, disbanding some and putting others into the army's command structure. With Teleki's appointment we also see more evidence of Horthy's shift away from the radical right wing forces that had swept him into power. Again, Bethlen

---

[65] Horthy, 133-137.
[66] Sakmyster, 60-61, 72.

turned down the job for the time being and recommended Teleki. That Horthy listened to Bethlen is key, because at this time Horthy had grown very frustrated with the parliamentary system and individuals like Pronay were urging him to mount a military coup. He could have easily had the support of the military for such an action as well as the support of a significant portion of the country, but Horthy stayed his hand, relying on the advice of Bethlen, a skilled statesman. This also bolsters the argument that Horthy was not purely driven by a desire for power.[67]

Teleki's term as prime minister, the first of two, also did not last particularly long, from July 1920 to the middle of April 1921. In that short span, however, several significant developments occurred. First, Teleki succeeded in curtailing the actions of the military detachments, as mentioned above, which proved key in regaining international recognition and ending a trade boycott. It was also under Teleki that the Hungarian government ratified the Treaty of Trianon—something Teleki managed to convince Horthy had to be done in order to normalize Hungary in international standing. This would not have been easy for the Horthy who had overseen Hungary's flags flown at half mast in response to the treaty's signing in Versailles (flags remained so until 1938,) as it in a sense validated the treaty in Hungary. His approval gave the members of parliament the ability to vote on it without fear of condemnation from him, and from a pragmatic point of view Hungary had no real choice but to do so. Horthy's personal position had not changed—he identified more with the members of the Awakening Magyars who angrily protested outside Parliament after the ratification, but he understood, or at least was swayed by those who understood, that there would be no hope of securing territorial revisions if Hungary did not first accept what had happened and become part of the international community again.[68]

During the Teleki regime, the rift between Horthy and the far right continued to grow. Pronay and other Szeged officers, disillusioned with Horthy, began to harshly criticize him. Horthy, ever caught between the two

---

[67] Romsics, 114-115; Sakmyster, 72-73
[68] Horthy, 136; Sakmyster, 73-74.

differing parts of the right, did still try to maintain ties with them, however, assuring them that they were not being abandoned, and that a fantastical plan to drive the Czechs out of Slovakia, utilizing Hungarian, German, and Polish forces, long in the planning, was postponed rather than cancelled. However, these reassurances were not enough for some, and in December 1920 Pronay decided to go ahead with the plan on his own to force Horthy's hand. However, they failed to keep the plans a secret and both the Hungarian and Czechoslovak governments found out well in advance. Horthy personally summoned Pronay and berated him for his foolishness. On the other hand, in 1921 Horthy himself proposed an equally fantastical plan that was rejected by both Teleki and his foreign minister, Gusztav Gratz. Later that year, however, Horthy abruptly switched his view and condoned talks with Czechoslovakia, and Teleki began the process of rapprochement. While this was a major shift for Horthy, and almost certainly influenced by his conservative advisors, the thought of regaining territory—through negotiation rather than military action—was still on his mind.[69]

In addition to the general stabilization of the country under Teleki's first term, Horthy's attitude toward governing was solidified as well. Despite his significant personal powers, Horthy would largely leave general policy decisions to his prime ministers, cabinet, and the parliament, slipping well into the role of constitutional monarch similar to his former liege-lord, Franz Joseph. Horthy was made aware of pending decisions, especially ones of great import, and would give his opinions in a spontaneous fashion, often appearing rather radical or naïve. However, as Sakmyster writes, Horthy's advisors quickly learned how to temper his fire, and Bethlen or Teleki would carefully explain the flaws in his ideas. More often than not, he would concede points to them, and it can be argued that Horthy understood that he lacked certain skills that made an adept politician, and thus declined to enforce his authority when he believed that his trusted advisors knew better. This again belies the argument that Horthy had a desire for power or sought to be a dictator, and lends credence to the idea that he was acting out of an old world

---

[69] Szucs and Szinai, 19-29; Sakmyster, 74-76.

sense of duty learned from his time as an officer in the Austro-Hungarian Empire.[70]

Another event of note that took place during Teleki's first brief term as prime minister is the most controversial, and something that has marred Teleki's otherwise favorable image in historiography: the passing of the *numerus clausus* law of 1920. Horthy, along with many Hungarians at the time, agreed that Hungary had a "Jewish problem." As discussed above, this problem only grew worse due to the two revolutions in Hungary after the war, specifically the communist revolution, despite efforts of the Jewish community to demonstrate that those Jews were a minority. Add to that the resentment toward the Jews, who were successful far beyond their percentage of the population, especially in the medical, law, journalism, and finance professions, the question changed from whether the Jews should be punished to how.[71] Teleki, while politically moderate and strongly opposed to the actions during the White Terror, shared in this feeling regarding Hungary's Jews, or at least large segments of the Jewish population, as did Horthy, and agreed that something should be done. Here we also see the differentiation among politicians like Horthy and Teleki between the "good Jews" and the "Galician Jews."[72] This view was used to justify the legislation, as technically not all Jews were targeted—and indeed they were not specifically mentioned in the legislation. The law, passed in September 1920, essentially stated that the percentages of students enrolled in universities had to be proportional to the percent of the population that they were. The Jews, who made up six percent of the population, were a far greater percentage of the university population, and thus the law impacted them almost exclusively.[73]

This law was the first piece of anti-Jewish legislation passed in post-World War I Europe, and it labeled Horthy and Hungary as antisemitic, and also set

---

[70] Sakmyster, 76-77.

[71] Sakmyster, 78-79.

[72] This term generally referred to Jews who had recently immigrated from Poland, and were thus not at all assimilated into Hungarian society, and more easily labeled as an unwanted foreign influence.

[73] Ezra Mendelsohn, *Jews of East Central Europe Between the World Wars* (Bloomington: Indiana University Press, 1983), 103-105; Sakmyster, 78-80.

two precedents for the new Hungary. First, this was a prime example of Horthy's regime taking an action that appears roughly in line with the views of the far right, but significantly divergent from their true wishes, in order to placate them, to "take the wind out of their sails." University students and staff, many of whom identified with the new far right, had clamored for this legislation, and its passing allowed the government to demonstrate to them that it was on their side regarding the Jews while in reality acting in a far more lenient manner. As we will see, this law was not strictly enforced, and within two years the percentage of Jewish students in universities rose back to over thirteen percent. Additionally, this law did little direct harm to the wealthy Jews with whom Bethlen and other members of the elite had close ties. They supported the regime, and the regime did not curtail their rights. As Ezra Mendelsohn explains, as undesirable as this position was for Hungarian Jews, it was preferable to the situation in Poland, where similar laws did not pass but popular antisemitic attitudes largely prevailed and Jews were more vulnerable to economic and civil prejudice. In fact, Hungary's Jewish leadership, which was incredibly patriotic, refused any attempts by foreign Jewish groups or international bodies to interfere with the passing of this law, which was in violation of a clause in the Treaty of Trianon, as they, like nearly all Hungarians, saw the despised treaty as an assault on Hungarian sovereignty, and did not want to grant it legitimacy by relying on it for their benefit.[74]

The second and more sinister legacy of this law was that it defined the Jews as a separate race differentiated from the Hungarian Magyar identity, a sharp change from the prewar attitude that saw Hungary's Jews as Magyars. Simultaneously, however, the regime still considered Hungarian Jews in the lost territories as Magyar, as it served a political purpose. This had little direct impact for some time, but the official separation of Jew and Magyar demonstrated the change in attitude and later on would lead to trouble.[75]

---

[74] Braham, 21-22; Mendelsohn, 104-105; Sakmyster, 79-80.
[75] Mendelsohn, 104-106.

Part 4: The Regent and the King

"Plans were put in hand for financial reconstruction, for new industries to combat the problem of unemployment. It looked as though we were following the right course. And then came the surprising news of His Majesty King Charles."[76] This is how Horthy, in his memoir, succinctly introduces the first attempt of Charles IV to reclaim his position as king of Hungary, at the tail end of a section detailing Hungary finally getting back in order and about to start rebuilding. This particular paragraph reads in a manner consistent with descriptions of his speeches, very off the cuff, and one can almost picture his bemused expression at hearing that news in 1921. The final major event of Teleki's short term as prime minister, Charles's attempted return, brought with it a challenge to the newly reorganized and recognized Hungary, and also a challenge to Horthy personally.

Horthy had always seen himself as completely loyal to the royal line, and, as regent, merely a steward until the time came that the king could return. There was at least some communication between Horthy and Charles as late as November 1920, when in a letter Charles expressed his confidence in Horthy and his hope that the regent would assist him in making overtures to the people and prepare the way for his eventual return.[77] When Horthy did not do so, and Charles grew impatient, he engineered his own return, and on Easter weekend, March 26 and 27, 1921, entered Hungary with a forged passport, concealing his identity. He made the decision to return with an overly optimistic sense of the political situation, and against the advice of his supporters as well as Horthy, all of whom knew that the rest of Europe would never consent to it. But the king was so confident that he did not even coordinate with the legitimists in Hungary, who staunchly supported his eventual return. He believed Horthy would quickly turn over power, and once the people saw his arrival, they would support him. He waved off the foreign complications by assuming that the major powers of Great Britain and Italy would not get involved, and he believed the French would support his

---

[76] Horthy, 137.
[77] Szucs and Szinai, 29-30.

claim when push came to shove. The successor states, he believed, would be angry and complain, but take no military action.[78]

This particular incident, to which Horthy devotes a fair amount of space in his memoir, seems to have made a particularly strong impression of Horthy as his description of events and actions taken fits well with the historical account as related by Sakmyster. Horthy first learned of the king's return after Charles had already reached Budapest from Count Antal Sigray, the Government Commissioner for western Hungary. Sigray briefed Horthy on the details of the king's arrival, and later learned that Prime Minister Teleki, who had happened to be in that region, had been informed early in the morning, after which he had hurried to Budapest to inform Horthy, but was delayed by car trouble (accounts vary from mechanical trouble to a directional failure), and thus only arrived after the king. Sakmyster adds that Teleki, who was just as conflicted over the issue as Horthy, and had been sent to ensure that Horthy did not consult officials like Gombos, who were staunchly opposed to a restoration of the royal line, may have deliberately arrived late to spare himself from having to take a side. Once informed, Horthy met with Charles at the palace, where he and his family were living. This unexpected situation is significant in understanding Horthy because in this instance he was caught off guard, and had to respond to the king on his own, without consulting any of his usual advisors. He was torn between his loyalty to the royal line, which he had sworn to serve as a member of the Austro-Hungarian Navy, and his duty to the new Hungary, to which he had also sworn loyalty. Plus, he was more aware of the international situation than Charles was. Horthy was flustered very early on, as he tried to tell Charles that he had to leave. We can also see Horthy's worry in his memoir, as he describes his thought process prior to meeting the king. Their meeting began amicably, but soured as Horthy tried in vain to convince the king that the political situation would not allow him to reclaim his position without dire consequences for Hungary.[79]

Eventually, Charles left, after he and Horthy came to a sort of détente,

---

[78] Sakmyster, 91.
[79] Horthy, 141-144; Sakmyster, 93-95.

with Horthy arguing that it would take time to arrange things and confer with the Great Powers, specifically France and Charles Briand, who Charles had named as sympathetic to his cause. The king, meanwhile, would lay low, and not announce his presence. Horthy's account concludes soon after this, with his confirming that the powers and Hungary's neighbors would in no way tolerate Charles's return. Charles eventually left Hungary on April 5, Horthy attributing it to an illness while other accounts hold that Charles deliberately delayed as he tried to make his plan work while Horthy tried to get him to leave quickly and quietly, lest an international incident erupt. Horthy also had to contend with the anti-Hapsburg segment of Hungarian society, which included the significant Smallholders party and the entirety of the far right. They wanted to arrest and forcibly expel Charles. This Horthy adamantly refused to do, as he still felt loyalty to Charles even as the would-be king was growing frustrated with the man he had thought would willingly and easily hand over the reins of power. In his memoir, Horthy emphasizes that he acted in the way he felt was best for the country, and that he never wore the medals or used the title Charles gave him in the hopes to change his mind. For all the heartache it caused him, however, Horthy's conduct during this crisis led him to be seen in a better light by other governments.[80]

Shortly thereafter, Teleki resigned from his position as prime minister, which suited Horthy just fine. Aside from the fact that he likely hoped to ask Bethlen once again, Teleki's ambiguous position during the attempt at return by Charles had shown him to be weak and/or not completely reliable in all respects. Furthermore, the day after Charles finally left, Teleki permitted the publication of Charles's manifesto, in defiance of the anti-legitimist Smallholders in the cabinet and parliament. Parliament then descended into loud, boisterous arguments, as legitimists and anti-legitimists, otherwise known collectively as free electors, went at each other. It was clear that Teleki was not going to be the man to fully consolidate and unify the country.[81]

---

[80] Horthy, 144-146; Sakmyster, 102-104; Macartney, 214.
[81] Sakmyster, 104; Deak, 22.

Part 5: The Bethlen Years

So, after twice turning down offers to become prime minister, Count Istvan Bethlen finally accepted Horthy's offer and became Horthy's third prime minister and Hungary's tenth since the war's end. He would remain in the position for over nine years, and he was so strongly in control that these years are sometimes referred to as the Bethlen era, with Horthy for the most part taking a back seat as Bethlen consolidated the regime's control and set about reorganizing and rebuilding the country.

Soon into his term, even as he set about trying to consolidate power, Bethlen faced an unexpected challenge, the second attempt of Charles IV to reclaim the throne. This time, Charles, no longer relying on Horthy, landed in secret in western Hungary, where he was joined by a group of his supporters. In an ironic twist, the day Charles returned, October 21, was the same day Bethlen gave a major speech announcing the formation of a Unified Party, and to accept in principle the eventual return of the king, as a conciliation to the legitimists. Charles, after his secret arrival, traveled with his armed supporters to the outskirts of Budapest, where they were met by an armed group of anti-Hapsburg students and far-right activists. There was a brief confrontation, after which Charles surrendered and was expelled from Hungary to the Madeira Islands, where he died the next year. A secondary impact of this attempted return was a clamp-down on prominent legitimist figures within Hungary which sent them firmly into the opposition, which would temporarily hamper Bethlen's consolidation program.[82]

Looking at this incident from Horthy's perspective adds more depth to the story, and further demonstrates the divisions in Hungarian society that Bethlen would dedicate his time in office to mending. Horthy, who maintains that he had been in contact with Charles but had not been informed of his return (likely because by this point Charles saw Horthy as illegitimate or at least as working against him), still does not show himself as resentful or angry

---

[82] Thomas Lorman, *Counter-Revolutionary Hungary, 1920-1925: Istvan Bethlen and the Politics of Consolidation* (Boulder, CO: East European Monographs, 2006), 77; Rothschild, 159; Seton-Watson, 190.

at the king, maintaining that he acted on bad advice given by legitimist figures in Hungary. Additionally, Horthy was hurt by the news that two officers who had been part of his circle in Szeged, Major Gyula Ostenberg and Colonel Anton Lehar, were among Charles's primary backers, providing the armed forces under their command. Horthy also mentions his dislike of the term legitimist, as he saw it as forcing a distinction between them and himself. He consistently saw himself as a supporter of the royal line and its return to Hungary when possible, and that the entire government, not a minority, had to recall him. Horthy also provides transcripts of a letter he sent Charles pleading with him to change his mind and not drag Hungary close to a civil war. His attempts to engage with the king diplomatically also did serve to slow down the legitimist advance and buy time for troops loyal to Horthy to meet them.[83]

Sakmyster adds that Horthy was torn even as he sent forces, because he did not want to see Hungarian fight Hungarian, and the Entente representatives had to strengthen his resolve, and sent a missive that made it clear that they were opposed to a Hapsburg return. And, of course, the successor states threatened war should that occur. Horthy recognized this as a greater threat, and strengthened his response. These actions render the argument that Horthy sought the crown for himself extremely flimsy. Following this crisis, Hungary passed a law officially dethroning the Hapsburg line, something that Horthy notes with sadness, and states that Hungary was forced to do so (though the country still officially remained a monarchy.) However, despite the initial wrinkles, Charles's attempted return played into Bethlen's hands, as it undermined the troublesome legitimist parliamentarians, and having just barely averted a civil war, consolidation would only look more appealing.[84]

Istvan Bethlen's involvement in the affairs of the new Hungary did not only begin with his appointment as prime minister. As mentioned previously, Bethlen was one of the counterrevolutionary leaders, having organized a group from Vienna in 1919, and was a close associate of Horthy throughout

[83] Horthy, 147-150; Sakmyster, 113.
[84] Sakmyster, 116-121; Horthy, 148, 151.

the counterrevolution and after. However, his work from 1921 to 1931, when he resigned, is what he is known for. His domination of this period was so complete that those who identified with the left displayed more enmity toward Bethlen than Horthy.[85]

Bethlen's goals, aside from the consolidation of government authority, was restoring a sense of order in the style of the prewar regime, which was liberal in some respects, but generally conservative. This is unsurprising, as Bethlen, the latest in a long aristocratic line, had been spent his formative years in the old regime. As a result, Bethlen, like most of the aristocracy, saw things in terms of class rather than race or religion—a key difference between the conservative, or "Horthy Right," and the radical right that would eventually become truly fascist in nature. This class struggle is also part of what set the two different segments of the right against each other, as we will see during the radical right's rise closer to the Second World War.[86]

However, we must not make the mistake of referring to Bethlen as a liberal in the modern sense, or even in the classical sense. Far from it. Among his first implemented policies was one that overturned a law passed under external pressure in 1920 that granted almost universal suffrage. Under the new law, only approximately twenty-seven percent of the population had the right to vote—Bethlen and Horthy both felt that the 1920 law was "too democratic." Furthermore, the open ballot was reinstituted in the more rural areas. Of course, the goals of these changes were to ensure that the government was able to maintain its power, and that people who were in his view more capable entered into positions of leadership. The masses could not be trusted. Later, during the 1930s and early 1940s, these policies would prove helpful in slowing the rise of the far right, which leads to the interesting question of whether, in such a case, limiting suffrage and using coercion to influence election results can be the lesser evil. These policies worked well, and the government party had a very comfortable majority in the 1922

---

[85] Bela Zsolt, *Nine Suitcases: A Memoir* (New York: Schocken Books, 2004), 4-5.

[86] Istvan Deak, "Hungary," in *The European Right: A Historical Profile,* ed. Hans Rogger and Eugen Weber (Berkeley: University of California Press, 1965), 364-365; Sakmyster, 104-150; Deak, 22-23; Romsics, 181.

election. In 1926, Bethlen reorganized the Upper House of parliament, determining of whom it would consist. These representatives included nobles, religious representatives (including rabbis), local representatives, representatives of key economic segments of society, universities, as well as personal appointees by Horthy. By its makeup, this chamber of parliament was also stacked heavily in favor of the conservative right, and due to the set nature of its appointees, less subject to the whims of the populace.[87]

Another key accomplishment of Bethlen's was his formation of a unified government party. Once it was formed, the party remained the dominant one in Hungary for essentially the entire Horthy period. Given the significant disparity between Hungary's leadership, the elites, and the general populace during this period, this this party was meant to cement an elite-based system of "qualified" people to run the country despite regular elections. Whether he made his decisions based on some sort of moral sense or simply out of a desire to remain part of the ruling class and ensure its dominance can be debated, but the fact remains that these changes he implemented, the limited suffrage, open ballot, and the upper parliamentary house with its designated representatives served as a bulwark against the popular, radical ideology that became more and more pervasive during the interwar period.

In his book, *Counter-Revolutionary Hungary, 1920-1925: Istvan Bethlen and the Politics of Consolidation* Thomas Lorman details the process by which Bethlen, over the course of those five years, succeeded in his goal. Bethlen took a country that was ideologically divided and still managed to largely achieve his goals, an act of skilled statesmanship. When he first assumed office, he did not even have a popular mandate. Instead of trying to win support from various parties for specific legislation, he went a step further in creating the unified party which, due to its nature, cancelled out many extreme views and resulted in moderate policies not directly linked to any particular political group. His priority was not to drive through a personal political agenda, but to provide a broad base of support for the central government.[88]

---

[87] Deak, 23-24; Romsics, 181-182; Sakmyster, 105.
[88] Lorman, 223-225.

Bethlen succeeded in retaining Hungary's legitimacy both internally and in the international arena, curtailing both the extreme right and extreme left (though the government was much harsher on the communists, as the party remained banned and its members were arrested), and managed a compromise that placated all parties after Charles IV's return and the near civil war that accompanied it. Bethlen also presided over the recovery of Hungary's economy (at least until the Great Depression) and knew when to pander to the more radical revisionists and when to work to improve relations with Hungary's neighbors and the international community. And it is must be noted that in Lorman's book, Miklos Horthy is referenced far fewer times, and when he is mentioned, Lorman notes that Bethlen had Horthy's complete backing even when Bethlen moved against the radical right, to the point that when Horthy's far-right associates, who had had his ear during the Szeged days and the aftermath of the counterrevolution, saw Horthy as almost subservient to the politically astute Bethlen. [89]

Under the Bethlen administration, life for Hungary's Jews notably improved. There were no anti-Jewish laws passed while Bethlen was prime minister, and the *numerus clausus* law already on the books was not strictly enforced; as a result, the percent of Jewish students in the university was again greater than the percentage of the Jewish population, though it was till lower than it had once been. Additionally, the government under Bethlen maintained close ties with the wealthy Jewish businessmen of Budapest, again demonstrating a more class-based view of the world rather than a religious or race-based one. During this period, however, Jews effectively could not become officers in the army or members of the bureaucracy. But these restrictions were not particularly damaging as the Jews affected by this had plenty of other ways to earn a living, as Hungarian Jewry was by and large better off than Jews elsewhere in Eastern Europe. Hungarian Jews were also much more integrated into society than in other nearby countries such as Poland. Hungarian Jews saw themselves as Hungarians "of the Mosaic faith," the emphasis on being Hungarian. There was virtually no Zionist movement

---

[89] Lorman, 226-228, 178, 176, 157,

in Hungary, and Hungarian Jews during the period overwhelmingly spoke Hungarian as opposed to Yiddish or German, and were generally just as nationalistic as Christian Hungarians. Even at the height of the antisemitic violence of the White Terror, Hungarian Jewish organization made very patriotic statements denouncing the Treaty of Trianon and stating their willingness to sacrifice for the fatherland. This is best exemplified by the fact that Hungarian Jews lodged no official protest against the *numerus clausus* law and in fact opposed protests by foreign Jewish organizations, as they did not want to grant legitimacy to the treaty by making use of it for their own gain. This disparity is definitely clear when looking at news clippings from the Jewish Telegraphic Agency, an international Jewish news and communication agency founded in 1917.[90] As with most Jews at the time, it was clearly left-leaning, and highly critical of Hungary under Horthy. Of course, even Jews in Hungary were by no means monolithic, and there was a notable trend among some younger Jews, specifically intellectuals like Oszkar Jaszi, who detested the Jewish establishment and oligarchs who supported the establishment, which that group hated politically.[91]

Overall, Hungary during the Bethlen years was quite stable, and things calmed noticeably after the wilder and emotionally charged years immediately after the war's end. Bethlen, with Horthy's blessing, managed to co-opt the Christian nationalist rhetoric of the far right (something that would become a common strategy for the regime in later years), declaring Hungary a

---

[90] "Numerus Clausus Will not Be Repealed in Hungary Until Lost Provinces Are Restored, Minister of Education Says," Jta.org, June 11 1924, http://www.jta.org/1924/06/11/archive/numerus-clausus-will-not-be-repealed-in-hungary-until-lost-provinces-are-restored-minister-of-educa; "Banffy Defends Restriction of Jewish Admissions," Jta.org, January 2, 1923, http://www.jta.org/1923/01/02/archive/banffy-defends-restriction-of-jewish-admissions; "Rothschilds, Kuhn Loeb & Co. Assailed for Aiding Hungary," Jta.org, May 17, 1923, http://www.jta.org/1923/05/17/archive/rothschilds-kuhn-loeb-co-assailed-for-aiding-Hungary; "Bethlen Reported to Have Decided on More Liberal Jewish Policy," Jta.org, March 6, 1924, http://www.jta.org/1924/03/06/archive/bethlen-reported-to-have-decided-on-more-liberal-jewish-policy.
[91] Mendelsohn, 105-111.

staunchly Christian nation, criticizing the influence of the "Jewish media," and defending the *numerus clausus* law in the face of international criticism. At the same time, the regime was staunchly conservative, did not enforce the *numerus clausus* law, and had good relations with wealthy Jews as well as with the Jewish establishment. It was the closest Bethlen and his supporters could come to recreating the prewar system that they idealized.[92]

However, this does not change the fact that Hungary's populace was still very sympathetic to the Christian nationalist message. During this period Christian unity (primarily between the two largest denominations, Catholics and Calvinists) was emphasized, and the Bethlen government took great pains to get the two denominations to make loyalty to the state paramount, so as to not argue over which should predominate, drawing on the injustices of Trianon to promote a message of unity. The conservative elite saw religion as a tool to both unify the people and to legitimize the government. Though the goal was not to make the state the center of life as it would become in fascist state, though it did become an integral part of society. And, as Paul Hanebrink writes, this system, which by its nature excluded Hungary's Jews, still managed to maintain order while their exclusion was rhetorical rather than actual. However, this reality would only be able to be maintained so long as the government's hold on power and its definition of Hungarian identity remained stable, and the extreme elements repressed. As we will soon see, the events of the 1930s would bring out feelings and actions that were dormant during this stable period.[93]

---

[92] Hanebrink, 109-110.
[93] Hanebrink, 113-115, 134-136.

CHAPTER 2
Shift To The Right And Into The German Orbit

Part 1: The Fall of Bethlen, the Rise of Gombos

Near the end of the 1920s, however, the Bethlen regime finally began to falter. Hungary began to feel the effects of the Great Depression in 1929, primarily due to the collapse of wheat prices, which hit one of Hungary's key exports hard. Things deteriorated further in May 1931, when Austria's *Creditanstalt* bank collapsed. Interestingly, this collapse happened right around new elections which returned Bethlen's government party to a strong position, and the effects truly hit the country shortly after. Hungary found itself unable to repay its creditors, who themselves were trying to withdraw all of their funds in panic. Hungary appealed to the League of Nations, which advised Hungary to balance its budget on its own via raising taxes, cutting salaries, cutting jobs, and stopping imports. This only made matters worse, and the entire agricultural class ended up nearly broke and in serious debt. As a significant portion of the population could no longer purchase goods, and was unable to sell exports or afford to import raw materials, the unemployment rate among the working class skyrocketed. This catastrophe eradicated the economic gains of the 1920s and threatened to undermine the consolidation that Bethlen had worked so hard to build. Bethlen resigned as prime minister in August of that year, and was replaced by another aristocrat of the same political mold, Count Gyula Karolyi. Karolyi endeavored to rectify the situation, following the dictates of the League of Nations closely, but the harsh economic measures only fueled more civil unrest. Workers demonstrated and went on strike, farmers revolted against the banks that were keeping them perpetually in debt, and the laid off civil service officials and army officers, along with university graduates who could not find work, all rose up in frustration. This anger allowed the radical right to again target the Jews, who were the majority of the creditors in Hungary, and who held a disproportionate amount of key positions in trade and industry, which led to many Christian Magyars feeling both that they had no way into these industries and that a minority group had too much economic influence. The movement continued to grow, as did the unrest, and Karolyi resigned just over a year later, in September 1932, unable to fight the multitudes of angry, frustrated people. On October 1 Horthy, yielding to public pressure, appointed the well known champion of the radical right, Captain Gyula Gombos, to the position of prime minister.[94]

Interestingly, however, while in the past Gombos had been vocal in his dislike of Jews, as his leadership position in the far right might imply, he made use of no such rhetoric during his tenure as prime minister. It was not because of a personal change of heart; as we will see, Gombos remained very much a far right political figure, and his ambitions and actions during his term bear that out. Rather, his avoidance of antisemitic rhetoric was a result of a deal made with Horthy. In exchange for appointment as prime minister, he agreed to tone things down so as to maintain the status quo that had been established during the Bethlen years. This is a fascinating development, and speaks to Horthy's newfound commitment to the conservative ideals that Bethlen and the old regime shared. It is also worth noting that Gombos, in addition to being the first truly far right prime minister since Horthy's appointment as regent, was also the first person without an aristocratic pedigree to hold the position. Gombos was in fact of German descent, and an attempt to prove he had a Hungarian noble heritage failed, much to his embarrassment. Seen through this lens, it is very easy to see Gombos's appointment as the point where the balance of power in Hungary began to shift toward the radical right, with Hungarians not of the conservative, aristocratic elite getting more of a voice, muzzled though Gombos was.[95]

---

[94] Macartney, 220-222.
[95] Seton-Watson, 193; Deak, 25-27.

The historical consensus makes it fairly clear that Gombos had definite authoritarian ideas, if not fascists ones, at least as far as governance was concerned. He particularly admired Italian dictator Benito Mussolini. On the other hand, some historians see parallels between Gombos's rise to power and that of the other major fascist leader of the era, Adolf Hitler. Both gained power while the country was in a deep economic crisis, promoted by governmental elites who hoped to maintain real power behind the scenes. Nandor Dreisziger adds that there is even evidence that Horthy and his advisors elevated Gombos to prime minister in the hope he would not be up to the task of managing the economic crisis, to ease tensions with the growing far right in Hungary and to politically end the career of a man who exemplified the unhealthy mix of military and politics that the establishment politicians feared. A more conservative successor was already in mind. Like Hitler, however, Gombos proved more politically adept than the elites anticipated, and Gombos almost succeeded in turning the tables by manipulating Horthy through flattery rather than the other way around. However, unlike Hitler, Gombos did not have a strong, organized power base behind him. Rather, he inherited the leadership of the conservative government party created by Bethlen, and Horthy did not let Gombos hold new elections upon coming into office. And while Gombos enjoyed great support among the radical right during his time in office despite his moderated tone, they understood that he was politically not strong enough to enact the sweeping "changing of the guard" as they had hoped. In fact, it would not be until 1935, not far from his own early death, that Gombos managed to craft a party in his image. Additionally, he never had a complete grip on Horthy, who still maintained close ties with Bethlen and other less radical political figures.[96]

That is not to say that Gombos was unable to accomplish some of his goals during his years as prime minister. He is considered by many the "father" of an axis—a term he coined in this use—consisting of Italy, Germany, and the Hungary he intended to transform; he sought to allay the friction that existed

---

[96] Dreisziger, 34-35; Macartney, 223; Hanebrink, 138.

between Italy and Germany (before Hitler's ascent.) This would allow Hungary to establish close ties with both, rather than having to maneuver between them. In his initial foreign policy aims, which included seeking support against the successor states for revision of the Treaty of Trianon and to gain support against the hated Soviet Union, Gombos was, in principle, in agreement with the Bethlen conservatives. However, that group desired better relations with Britain more so than with Germany, and Dreisziger makes an interesting distinction between Horthy, who as a navy man gravitated toward Britain, while Gombos, and army man, was more drawn to Germany.[97]

Under Gombos, the economic situation began to improve, helped by both a reduction of imports and with a friendly neighbor in Germany now a key trading partner of Hungary. During the early 1930s industrialization increased in Hungary as well. In foreign policy, Gombos first strengthened Hungary's ties to Mussolini's Italy, building on the already in place pact of friendship, which later added Austria. In 1934, Hungary, Italy, and Austria signed the Rome Protocols, which solidified this pseudo-alliance. This was largely an economic agreement, focused on economic reconstruction in the Danubian region; mutual trade, and ease of transport. However, the Protocols meant different things to the different groups involved. Engelbert Dollfuss, the head of the Austrian government, saw it as a bulwark against Hitler and against the growing national-socialist movement in Austria. Some in Hungary saw it in a similar light, aimed at keeping Germany out of Austria; however, others, including Horthy, saw it as a response to the Pact of Organization signed by the Little Entente—the successor states—and the Balkan League earlier in 1934. To still others in Hungary, the Protocols were simply economic agreements. Hungary definitely profited from these arrangements despite some friction within the bloc; politically it helped strengthen Hungary in regard to its belligerent neighbors, and the economic provisions seem to have done much to help Hungary's agricultural industry through the depression period. And, finally, while ultimately Austria would join with Germany, the Protocols arguably kept Austria independent longer.[98]

---

[97] Dreisziger, 34-35; Macartney, 222-223.
[98] Dreisziger, 38-40; Seton-Watson, 194.

At the same time, the Gombos administration set out to improve Hungary's ties with Nazi Germany. Setting aside ideological sympathies, closer ties with Germany were advantageous for several reasons. First, it gave Hungary additional political support in the region, counteracting the successor states. Second, it made it so Hungary did not have to rely completely on Italy, politically or economically. Germany, as a growing industrial nation, was also an ideal trading partner; Germany was a good market for Hungary's agricultural products, and Hungary sought German industrial goods. But the ideological considerations were also important. Gombos, who, in 1933, became the first foreign leader to meet with Hitler, greatly admired the Nazi state's organization, both in a military and economic sense. Other Hungarian leaders, including Horthy, had misgivings, however, especially after the Rohm purge on June 30, 1934, and the murder of Engelbert Dollfuss on July 25. Hungarian-German relations were also complicated by Hungary's sizeable German minority. Particularly with Germany's re-emergence as a significant power under Hitler, this minority became very much identified with Germany, and Germany itself sent visitors disguised as tourists, who spread pan-German and National Socialist ideas among Hungary's German population. However, the economic advantages of the Hungarian-German relationship proved strong enough to ensure ties remained good. By the end of Gombos's time in office, ties with Germany had progressed to the point where talks were held regarding "actions" of varying kinds against Czechoslovakia, but Gombos could not push things further due to his poor health.[99]

Even as his health failed, Gombos refused to resign his post, and in October 1936 he died. Much of Hungary's political elite was quietly relieved at this development, while Gombos's supporters, mourned the early death of a "Hungarian aspirant to Fuhrerdom." While his premature death put and end to any ambition by Gombos to become such a leader, his four years in office had the lasting legacy of bringing Hungary into the German orbit, as well as energizing Hungary's radical right, which would play a major role in Hungary for the rest of the Horthy era.[100]

---

[99] Dreisziger, 40-46.
[100] Dreisziger, 48-49; Seton-Watson, 194-195.

Following Gombos's death, Hungary had two more prime ministers in office for comparatively short periods before the advent of World War II. The first, Kalman Daranyi, was more of a conservative and focused more on domestic issues; the key piece of legislation passed during his short term, which among other things introduced the secret ballot to rural districts, was passed with broad multiparty support. Foreign issues did not get resolved as easily for Daranyi, and for his first year in office Germany butted heads with his government regarding the treatment of Hungary's Germans. In November 1937, however, Daranyi, along with Foreign Minister Kalman Kanya, visited Berlin and the friction was smoothed over. Additionally, Hitler again implied that if Hungary participated when Germany acted against Czechoslovakia, it could regain some lost territory. Hungary was split over this issue; the army was very much in favor of military cooperation, while the political class was more wary. The conservatives, including Horthy, sought alternative possibilities; closer ties were forged with Poland, and a renewed campaign was launched to impress on Great Britain the justice of Hungary's revisionist aims. However, the foreign situation grew more difficult as Hitler's Germany increased its influence. In 1936, Germany occupied the Rhineland, and by the end of that year, Italy, which Hungary was hoping to use as a counterbalance to Germany in the Danube region, moved closer to Germany. Furthermore, the signs of the impending *Anschluss* of Austria grew ever clearer, and just before the end of Daranyi's term, Austria became a part of the Reich. What ultimately sank the Daranyi government, however, were his attempts to reach an agreement with the far right Arrow Cross.[101] In late 1937 and early 1938, Daranyi's government adopted lesser versions of several Arrow Cross demands, including a new progressive income tax, increased military spending, and new anti-Jewish legislation. These concessions, and secret negotiations, were designed to "take the wind out of the sails of the

---

[101] The Arrow Cross Party, founded and led by Ference Szalasi as the Party of National Will in 1935, was the most significant National Socialist party in Hungary, modeled after Germany's Nazi Party. It was extremely nationalistic, pro-Catholic, anti-capitalist, anti-communist, antisemitic, and at odds with the Horthy administration throughout its existence.

antisemites," to quote Daranyi. However, Horthy was vehemently opposed to any concession to or rapprochement with the Arrow Cross, and was furious with Daranyi, firing him in May 1938.[102]

Daranyi's replacement was Bela Imredy, known primarily for his knowledge of economics; he had previously been president of the National Bank and had served as a minister without portfolio, where he assisted in coordinating economic policy. While it was Horthy, as usual, who appointed Imredy, he did so on the advice of Bethlen and other conservatives. Imredy was known to have good British connections and sympathies more with the west than with Germany. At the same time, Imredy exemplifies the rightward shift Hungary was undergoing at this late stage. Initially, he did maintain a cautious relationship with Germany—and the Germans were as harsh with him as with Daranyi—and took action against Ferenc Szalasi, the leader of the far right Arrow Cross, sentencing him to a prison sentence. Almost ironically, however, this act against the Arrow Cross only strengthened Szalasi politically, making him a martyr of sorts, and allowed Germany to more directly influence the Hungarian fascists. Not long into his term, Imredy would abruptly change course, proving far more open to German overtures. In light of the 1938 Munich crisis,[103] which showed that promises made by the western powers could not necessarily be relied on, along with the fact that alliance with Germany could lead to the recovery of territory by Hungary,[104] Imredy and many other Hungarians became willing collaborators. Among his first actions following this, Imredy replaced Foreign Minister Kalman Kanya,

---

[102] Macartney, 226-227; Dreisziger, 50-53; Stanley G. Payne, *A History of Fascism, 1914-1945* (Madison: University of Wisconsin Press, 1995), 274; Istvan Deak, *Hungary from 1918 to 1945* (New York: Columbia University, Institute on East Central Europe, 1986), 29.

[103] Often referred to as the Munich Agreement, it was an agreement permitting Nazi Germany's annexation of the region known as the Sudetenland, which had been a part of Czechoslovakia.

[104] This was known as the First Vienna Award. With the approval of both Germany and Italy, on November 2, 1938, Hungary received significant territory from Slovakia and Ruthenia, an area known in Hungary as the Felvidek. This approximated one fifth of the territory lost to Czechoslovakia.

who had long been an irritation to the Germans, with the much more pro-German Count Istvan Csaky.[105]

The Magyars in the recovered regions, worried about how their economic status would be affected by becoming part of Hungary, pushed for increased anti-Jewish restrictions (a law had been passed already during Imredy's term, but it had been prepared under Daranyi). Imredy proved quite willing to comply, and also began to consider implementing land reform. At the same time, he formed his own far right organization. As before, Horthy and the still strong conservative elite reacted strongly to this rightward shift and had Imredy replaced. The manner of Imredy's forced resignation is notable. As part of his anti-Jewish legislation, the definition of what made one a Jew became more stringent. Imredy's enemies, many of whom opposed the law, nevertheless made use of it, producing documents alleging that Imredy had a Jewish ancestor, which prompted him to resign in embarrassment in February 1939.[106]

Part 2: The Radicalization of Hungarian Society

While both the preceding decade and the aftermath of World War I played important roles in charting the course Hungary took to and through World War II, the 1930s are by far the most significant. Yes, Hungary was arguably gripped by a more fervent far right mindset during the counterrevolution, conservative authoritarian rule during the Bethlen administration in the 1920s suppressed the far right elements within Hungary and consolidation unified the country. By the 1930s, however, Hungary started down a path that it would remain on, moving ever rightward, until the deposing of Horthy by the Germans and the installation of a true fascist government. As several historians note, it was during this decade that those suppressed radical ideas re-emerged in many significant segments of Hungarian society. And this sentiment, accompanied by antisemitism, was not confined to some marginalized, if large, group within Hungary.

---

[105] Rothschild, 178-179.
[106] Rothschild, 179-180; Macartney, 228-229.

This trend was seen among the poorer smallholders, but also among more well-off groups in Hungary. One such group was the army, specifically its officers. Things had already changed significantly with the war's end, as Hungary's armed forces were no longer part of the larger Austro-Hungarian military, where they were a minority. Many officers were involved in the counterrevolution in 1919, and unsurprisingly were strongly in favor of revision by any means necessary. After this, the army began to reorganize and work on plans to regain Hungary's lost territory, and these young officers grew extremely ambitious, to the point that they would take the initiative in both foreign and domestic matters. They were the strongest voices calling for reclaiming territory from the successor states by force. And while men like Horthy, Bethlen, and Teleki shared similar desires, they were too pragmatic to consider such rash plans made by inexperienced officers, and carefully disassociated themselves from the elements of the army that had participated in atrocities during the White Terror. Particularly with Bethlen and Teleki, the road to territorial revision was a long, gradual one, and more emphasis had to be put on restoring the country to prosperity and domestic stability. Horthy was somewhat of a different matter, having been a military man for almost all of his life. He retained close ties with the military during his time as regent, occupying the space between the conservative aristocracy and the more radical military. Horthy even went further along with the military on some occasions, being easily riled by talk of combating Bolshevism, and lent support to several aggressive military plans which never came to fruition.[107]

And yet, Horthy himself realized that these grandiose plans were impractical, bringing him into close alignment with Bethlen. Additionally, as per the dictates of the Treaty of Trianon, Hungary's army was downsized and many of the younger, more radical officers were demobilized, with the army's general staff of senior officers largely made up of more conservative men who were against the army interfering in politics and content with Bethlen's course. As with the general right wing mood, however, the radical right was dormant, not truly suppressed. This lull and normalization of the

[107] Thomas Sakmyster, "Army Officers and Foreign Policy in Interwar Hungary, 1918-1941," *Journal of Contemporary History 10*, no. 1 (1975): 19-22.

government-military relationship was not to last. Many of these officers came from a middle-class background, and when they were demobilized they went into key governmental and industrial positions, while remaining in close contact with their military friends. Gyula Gombos was emblematic of this group, and according to Sakmyster, it was his appointment as prime minister that was the turning point for Hungary's military establishment during this period. As described in brief above, Gombos's ambitious plan during his tenure entailed transforming Hungary into a more fascistic state similar to Mussolini's Italy[108] and Hitler's Germany. As Sakmyster notes, he failed in that, both due to his death in 1936 and due to growing opposition to his unsubtle plans. However, he had much success in reshaping the country's military. By 1935, most of the top army positions were occupied by men politically loyal to Gombos, and by 1936 most military officers in general were of radical right orientation, sympathetic to Hungary's fascist neighbors. This right-wing bent only grew more pervasive as the cadets trained in Hungary's Ludovika Academy, a military college, were fed the far right ideology by their instructors. Additionally, the idea that the military was meant to play a political role in society became more widespread. According to Sakmyster, this is evidenced by the practice of sending military attaches sent abroad, who would on occasion encroach on diplomatic and political activity that was meant to be only handled by the diplomats.[109]

This shift in the military was also driven by the types of people who enlisted. A significant number were from the lower middle class, which Sakmyster points out is a social group throughout Europe at the time that was particularly susceptible to fascism. Additionally, many officers came from non-Magyar backgrounds, most often German, as it was a decent career path that was open to them as a minority. Even before Gombos's rise to power, Hungarian military officers often had close ties to their German counterparts, drawing on the experiences of the First World War as well as a shared hatred of communism, not to mention the sense of kinship that Hungarian officers of German descent had with German officers. However, they did not attempt

---

[108] Hungary formally allied itself with Italy in 1927.
[109] Sakmyster, "Army Officers," 22-23.

to interfere in political matters while Gombos was in power, as he was in essence their representative, but during his time in office the relationship between the two militaries grew even stronger, and after Gombos drew Hungary closer to Germany, more Hungarian officers had a chance to observe both German military and political leaders, and liked what they saw— particularly in relation to Germany's aggressive military policy toward Czechoslovakia, the most hated of the successor states in Hungary. Later in the 1930s, when war seemed on the horizon, these officers would push for rearmament so the country could participate and be capable of securing territorial revision. After Gombos's death, however, the political elites, Horthy included, began to pull back from the radical course Gombos had set, something the radicalized officers took note of. This led to conflict between the government and the military, and the rift continued to grow up until the outbreak of war, as the general staff of the military, including Chief of Staff Jeno Ratz, continued to push for rearmament and began to propose political changes, something completely outside his official responsibility. Another official, Dome Sztojay, former general staff officer and Hungary's ambassador to Germany (and future prime minister), later took matters into his own hands, holding unauthorized military talks with Germany regarding possible military campaigns.[110]

To that end, the radicalized officers again turned to Horthy, appealing to the "Szeged spirit" of the counterrevolutionary days. However, despite many attempts, and one instance where Horthy almost went along with a plan to attack Czechoslovakia, Horthy heeded the advice of his conservative advisors, greatly frustrating the radical officers. In 1938, he gave a speech where he voiced his opposition to the army involving itself in political matters.[111] Later that year, however, Hungary did begin rearmament, placating the officers somewhat, but then, in the aftermath of the Austrian *Anschluss*, Horthy's government, rebuffed a German offer of returned territory on the condition that Hungary take part in an attack on Czechoslovakia. At this time there was also division among high ranking officers in the army, as some opposed action

---

[110] Sakmyster, "Army Officers," 23-27.
[111] Szucs and Szinai, 97-99.

on the grounds that they did not feel the army was sufficiently ready for any significant action. We will leave the drama of Hungary's radicalizing army here, to be picked up with the advent of World War II, but the fact of the intense radicalization is something that must be accounted for as we approach the outbreak of war itself, and Hungary's eventual involvement.[112]

In addition to the military, many Hungarians in important professions, including doctors, lawyers, and engineers, became radicalized during the interwar period. As Maria Kovacs notes, previously members of these professions had been politically liberal and not too concerned with politics. During these decades, they became extremely politicized, attracted to radical ideologies on both the right and left. Kovacs writes that this radicalization first occurred after the collapse of Austria-Hungary in 1918, when professional groups took advantage of the power vacuum to advance radical idea in both the Karolyi and Kun revolutions and governments. These revolutions were both products of the left, of course, but still significant as they represented the entry of such people into the realm of politics. The radical leftist bent of many members of these professions, naturally, led to a backlash once the communist revolution collapsed, and the surge of antisemitism during the White Terror thrust the professions into the political arena (Kovacs focuses on engineers specifically). In 1919, a right wing organization was founded within the profession, and among its demands was a prioritization of Christian engineers over Jewish ones. By the early 1920s, an engineering organization set up by the government had the power to police engineers on a political basis, potentially denying them the right to practice their profession. And despite Hungary's shift to the more moderate conservative right in the 1920s, radicalization continued; in 1920 an organization called *Hungaria* was established as a "right-wing paramilitary fraternity at Budapest's Technical University."[113] One membership requirement was certification that all of one's relatives, going back to

---

[112] Sakmyster, "Army Officers," 26-29.
[113] Maria Kovacs, "The Ideology of Illiberalism in the Professions: Leftist and Rightist Radicalism Among Hungarian Doctors, Lawyers and Engineers, 1918-1945," *European History Quarterly 21*, no. 2 (1991): 192.

grandparents, had been properly baptized. Many of this organization's leaders earned important positions by the early 1930s, with some serving in parliament, some in Gyula Gombos's government, and others in the re-emerging far right organizations. By the late 1930s, the engineering profession became increasingly antisemitic as Jews continued to be successful in the profession, and by 1938 the politics of the radical engineering groups, revolved almost solely around implementing antisemitic legislation.[114]

The radicalization path for doctors during the interwar period differed somewhat from that of the engineers. Concerns of the medical industry stemmed from previous issues involving industrialization as well as the advent of eugenics research, and worry of the Magyar race not being harmed as medical care became more widely available. Like most radical ideologies, this focus on race took on a collectivist bent, the larger group taking precedence over individual liberties. During the communist revolution, medical care became socialized, and left-leaning doctors were called on to assume political roles to transform society according to the ideals of the revolution. There were professional purges of anticommunist professionals and nuns, and revolutionary officials without medical education were made heads of hospitals. Hungary's doctors followed a path similar to that of the engineers, moving rightward, eventually founding the antisemitic National Union of Hungarian Doctors, which played a role in the passing of the *numerus clausus* law. Later, under Bethlen, Hungary followed the path pre-war Hungary had been on, instituting a centralized health insurance system and welfare program. This, too, was co-opted by far-right elements, and progressives, women, and Jews were excluded from high ranking official positions. The far right also seized upon the idea of eugenics and used it to keep out corrupting "revolutionary lineages." This race-based ideology put them starkly at odds with the conservatives in the government, such as Bethlen and even Horthy in this case, who saw the world through a class based lens, as we have discussed.[115]

During the Depression years, the far right only grew more hostile to the

[114] Kovacs, 190-193, 196-197.
[115] Kovacs, 198-202.

Jews. Because Jews were not permitted to work in the state-run insurance program, rather as private doctors, they were ironically sheltered from much of the impact of the economic crash. As Kovacs says, it is of little surprise that the far-right union became a central part of the emerging fascist movement, lobbying for stricter anti-Jewish laws and more collaboration with fascist Nazi Germany.[116] Understanding just how radicalized Hungarian professionals had become is key to understanding the later rise of the radical right and how it was able to so drive Hungary's path despite not holding power. Hungary's radical right was not just made up of lower class malcontents, it had support in all areas of society, especially by the late 1930s.

Part 3: Gombos's Machinations; Attempts to Chart a Different Course

When Horthy first mentions Gombos in his memoirs, he writes that from their first meeting at Szeged in 1919, he noted both good and not so good qualities in Gombos, who at the time was a young army captain. Horthy does not elaborate on these overmuch, but notes that he saw Gombos as an excellent officer and orator, but he disapproved of his appointing young officers who held similar views to him, encouraging political leanings that Horthy did not share. Horthy also compares Gombos to Hitler and Mussolini, stating that the models of both dictators was something that inspired Gombos. Of course, it is difficult to tell if these were thoughts Horthy held in 1932 or if he wrote with hindsight in this matter. The only time-bound statement Horthy makes initially is that he was somewhat hesitant to appoint Gombos, and made the decision after consulting with Bethlen and other trusted politicians. Unfortunately, there is not much more available in the way of primary sources to let us better see the nature of their relationship. There is a document that is a recording of the minutes of a 1932 cabinet session at which Horthy and Gombos were both present, as well as a letter sent from Horthy to Gombos in 1933. The documents' translators,

---

[116] Kovacs, 203.

Szucs and Szinai, argue in their analysis and description of these sources that they demonstrate a strong alliance between Horthy and Gombos, but a reading of the documents in question does not conclusively show this. Secondary sources written by accredited historians (neither Szinai nor Szucs, appear to have any accreditation as historians) all indicate that Horthy and Gombos did not see eye to eye on a number of issues.[117]

Of particular note is an assertion by Szucs and Szinai, that Horthy and Gombos conspired to hold new elections which would allow Gombos to control the parliament. However, Horthy did not allow this to happen until 1935, almost three full years after Gombos took office. In his memoir, Horthy writes that he eventually allowed this because he felt that the prime minister he appointed to should have his loyalty, at least up to a point, and that in order to effectively govern the prime minister should have a majority in parliament. This line of thinking is very much in keeping with Horthy's old-world view of things: Gombos had done well during his first years, had kept his word regarding the Jews, and it was clear he had public support. He had also overseen an increase in Horthy's own power. Szucs and Szinai do accurately note, however, the fact that Horthy authorized the dissolution of parliament on his own, without consulting Bethlen. Yes, Horthy did feel a sense of loyalty to Gombos, and gave him leave to hold elections that ultimately led Hungary further down the far-right path, but without surviving documents on what exactly went though his mind at this time, we can only judge based on what we know, namely that Horthy did not act out of agreement with all or most of Gombos's policy decisions, and that the old-world ideas of loyalty and governance that he describes is in line with what we do know about Horthy.[118]

A second key issue that deserves additional attention is Hungary's foreign policy during this period, something which could fill an entire book on its own. As mentioned above, it was largely on Gombos's initiative that Hungary's ties with Germany grew stronger during this period. As of his assumption of the office of the prime minister, Hungary's only ally via treaty

---

[117] Horthy, 166-167; Szucs and Szinai, 61-68; Sakmyster, 178-179.
[118] Horthy, 166-167; Szucs and Szinai, 64-65; Sakmyster, 179-181.

was Mussolini's Italy; Italy was still considered a great power, and Mussolini lent vocal support to Hungary's revisionist aims. However, even in the late 1920s when this treaty was signed by Bethlen's government, he knew that an alliance with Hungary's other large neighbor, Germany, made sense, though he did not actively pursue one during his time in office. Even after Gombos visited Germany's new chancellor, Adolf Hitler, and forged close ties with Nazi Germany, many in Hungary's political elite were wary of Germany gaining too much influence in the region. Furthermore, they worried about Gombos's plans, and the conservative elites, for the most part, did not favorably view the new German ruling class.[119]

One significant figure who held this view and played a key role in Hungary's attempts to mitigate German influence was Foreign Minister Kalman Kanya. Kanya, like Bethlen and much of the rest of Hungary's political elite, was ideologically conservative, a man of the old order. Appointed to head the foreign ministry by Gombos in 1933, Kanya had previously served as the Hungarian minister in Berlin. What made Kanya unique, however, was that due to having largely lived abroad in service of the Hapsburg monarchy for most of his adult life, he had a broader perspective of Europe, not a purely Magyar-centric one. This allowed him to approach issues facing Hungary from an "outsider's" perspective, and he was largely immune to the emotional nationalism that spurred the growth of the far right. Of course, he favored at least some sort of revisionism, but he was pragmatic rather than emotional. He recognized early on that, given Hungary's position, they could not be too ambitious. He also strongly opposed the idea of Hungary directly and strongly linking itself to one particular country or bloc. Rather, Hungary should maintain a "free hand" in the political scene, and avoid making a binding military or political commitment to any country. Hungary would accept help from the great powers, and make small deals, but avoid major, long-term arrangements. This was especially true, in his view, starting in 1936, when the blocs that would become the Axis and the Allies began to form.[120]

---

[119] Thomas Sakmyster, *Hungary, the Great Powers, and the Danubian Crisis, 1936-1939* (Athens: University of Georgia Press, 1980), 34-35, 44-45, 54.
[120] Sakmyster, *Danubian Crisis*, 54-57.

Despite having been appointed by Gombos, Kanya felt little loyalty to him, and despite having been Hungary's minister in Berlin, during which time he was thought of as very pro-German, he was decidedly repulsed by the new Germany that arose with Hitler. Privately, he had very harsh words for Hitler and his inner circle. Publicly, of course, he remained diplomatic and avoided direct clashes with Germany while trying to keep it at arm's length, which also necessitated restraining Gombos until the latter's death in 1936. Kanya was very much a traditionalist as well in the way he viewed people; he detested the idea of military officer taking on the role of politicians, and preferred the "old way" of foreign policy; competent, elite statesmen making decisions behind the scenes, rather than pandering to the uneducated masses.[121]

Kanya remained active in seeking alternative solutions during this period, with full support from Bethlen, Horthy, and other conservatives, as he sought to first improve ties with Great Britain, and later, as the likelihood of an Austrian *Anschluss* grew, to even consider a Hapsburg restoration in Austria (and possibly Hungary) as a means to form a Danubian bloc against the growing German influence. This plan, as well as future plans for Danubian cooperation, were hampered by a number of factors, including German and Italian opposition, an unwillingness by the Western European powers to get involved, and strong reluctance by all Hungarians to come to a rapprochement with the successor states. However, in 1936 and 1937, Hungary, then under the Daranyi administration, brought up the possibility of an agreement, walking a fine line to avoid angering the Germans and Italians. The possibility of a deal between Hungary, Czechoslovakia, and Austria came closer to realization in late 1937 and early 1938, but it was already too late, and plans did not come to fruition. And of course the *Anschluss* in March 1938 took Austria completely out of the game.[122]

Hungary's last gambit to form a bloc to resist German influence while not directly opposing Germany was to form an agreement with Poland, with

---

[121] Sakmyster, *Danubian Crisis*, 67-69.

[122] Dreisziger, 60-69; Sakmyster, *Danubian Crisis*, 58-59; Betty Jo Winchester, "Hungary and the 'Third Europe'" *Slavic Review 32*, no. 4 (1973): 744-748.

which Hungary had historical ties, not to mention the fact that both wanted to slow the spread of German influence, and both detested communism and the Soviet Union. Throughout 1937 and 1938, the countries grew closer and adopted similar approaches to the political situation, and there were talks of forming a Danube-Vistula axis, an alliance of several East-Central European states. Ultimately, however, little of consequence came of these attempts. While much can be said regarding these complex negotiations, which also included Italy and Great Britain, it goes far afield from the main point that Hungary's conservative elites attempted to avoid falling completely under the sway of the ascendant Nazi Germany while still wishing to further the goal of territorial revision. At the same time, however, the growing far right, which by this point included much of the army, pushed for closer ties to Germany, putting pressure on the government.[123]

In his memoir, Horthy does not discuss these negotiations in detail, though he does touch on some related aspects, such as his misgivings about Hitler, and that he did not meet with Hitler while Germany and Austria were at odds. He does, however, admit that at first Hitler was easy to speak to and a "delightful host," at least as of their first meeting in 1936. Indeed, a memorandum he wrote prior to the meeting containing potential topics for discussion seems quite average, if long-winded. Horthy also mentions Hungary's historical ties to Poland, and describes their common aims as well as his visit there in 1938.[124] John Flournoy Montgomery, the American minister to Hungary during this period, also makes reference to some of the worries of Hungary's ruling class about German influence in the mid 1930s, mentioning Kanya in particular. Flournoy lays at least some of the blame for failing to check Germany's growing influence on Great Britain, France, and the successor states, particularly in regard to Hitler's annexation of Austria. In light of this evidence, it is hard to argue that Hungary's ruling class wished for closer ties with Germany, even as the mood of much of the country, and some people in positions of leadership, shifted that way.[125]

---

[123] Dreisziger, 72-79.
[124] Horthy, 174-175, 184-186; Szucs and Szinai, 82-90; Sakmyster, 190-191.
[125] Montgomery, 80-81, 90-93.

Finally, we must take one additional look at the social situation in Hungary during this period, in particular in regard to Hungary's Jewish population. With the far right on the rise not just in Hungary, but throughout central and eastern Europe, changes were inevitable. Simply put, things began to deteriorate with the advent of the Great Depression. Economic trouble naturally fueled anger among those hardest hit, and in particular Ezra Mendelsohn mentions Hungary's sizeable German minority. Due to their natural ties to Germany, they were among the first groups in Hungary to embrace Nazism once Hitler rose to power, which only added to their already present antisemitic feelings. This shift is more significant than it might sound because of the German minority's strong presence in the military. Gyula Gombos himself was partially of German descent, and there was considerable anxiety just prior to his taking the prime minister position. And while he most certainly pulled Hungary in a rightward direction, and forged close ties with Hitler's Germany, to the surprise of everyone there did not appear to be any significant change in the status quo as far as the Jews were concerned during his time in office.[126]

As a result of Gombos's abrupt shift, he actually had good relations with the Jewish establishment and elites, which interestingly put him at odds with his natural allies in the far right. Shifting toward the center, in action if not in ideology, did, however, prompt the growth of the fascist Arrow Cross Party under the leadership of Ferenc Szalasi. And while Gombos may have proven less radical than many had dared to hope, the far right continued to assert itself, and the administrations that followed, Imredy's in particular, found themselves more and more influenced by these forces. Mendelsohn does point out that this was by no means a monolithic trend, as the older, more tolerant views were still to be found in some segments of society, including many of the conservative elites. But the greater trend of growing antisemitism was there to stay.

Paul Hanebrink goes into more detail regarding this growing trend. As mentioned earlier, many people who worked in the civil service and major

---

[126] Mendelsohn, 112-114.

professions, whose social standing was harmed in the aftermath of the war, gravitated toward the seemingly successful National Socialist Party that had arisen in Germany, and were disappointed that the 1919 counterrevolution had not led to something similar in Hungary. During the two postwar decades, these far-right Christian nationalists still hoped to achieve some major change, and cleanse Hungary of the "Judeo-Bolshevik spirit." Gombos's abrupt about-face was extremely disappointing to these people. They still supported him politically, but they no longer saw him as the man who would enact a "changing of the guard" in the political system.[127]

There were several movements that cropped up, but most were short-lived and sectarian, made up of only a small, specific group such as rural farmers and military officers. The one that remained steady, however, was Szalasi's Arrow Cross Party, which by the late 1930s became the largest opposition party in Hungary. Hanebrink relates that in 1937 Arrow Cross members streamed through Budapest with leaflets, proclaiming their imminent rise to power, to the point that people began to fear a coup attempt. With the far right exercising significant power in parliament and with the prospect of revision via an alliance with Germany tantalizingly close, pressure mounted on the Hungarian government to act on the "Jewish Question."

In 1938, as a result, Prime Minister Daranyi promoted the first Jewish law since the 1920 *numerus clausus*, even before Germany returned land to Hungary via the First Vienna Award (though it would not become law until after Daranyi was replaced by Bela Imredy.) This law set quotas on the numbers of Jews in several major professions and declared that the old *numerus clausus* law was to be properly enforced. There were still some exemptions, namely Jews who had converted to Christianity prior to the white Terror, veterans of the First World War, and the wives and children of Jews killed during the war. The Daranyi government justified this in several ways; the fact that Jews were grossly overrepresented in these fields, that this law was to reassure the country's Jews that this was the worst that would happen—they need not fear Hungary acting as Germany had in recent years,

---

[127] Mendelsohn, 114-115; Hanebrink, 137-138.

likely referring to the Nuremberg Laws of 1935—and that most Jews had not properly become Magyarized, and therefore did not merit equal legal treatment. Jewish groups protested strongly, particularly against the last of the three rationalizations, declaring the law un-Hungarian in character, and stated that the Jews *were* true, loyal Magyars. The Jewish establishment's response was worded quite strongly, which marked a shift it its usual cautious manner.[128]

The law was hotly debated in parliament, with its opposition arguing that it sounded like something "made in Germany," created purely to appease the Nazi state. Others who argued against it pointed to the disparity between the treatment of the Jews and the German minority in Hungary. The Jews, unlike the Germans, were being told that their "failure to assimilate," was costing them their equal status while the Germans were allowed to remain true to their ethnic background despite also being disliked by many Hungarian nationalists. Of course, the fact that Nazi Germany had taken up "the cause" of German minorities outside of Germany likely factored into this decision. Despite the objections, the law still passed, with even some conservative elites, such as Count Pal Teleki, supporting it, as well as the Catholic church. It should be noted, however, that like the old *numerus clausus* law, it was not racist, unlike the German antisemitic legislation, which allowed for no exceptions. Supporters also argued that the law was necessary to appease external forces without going too far.

Unfortunately, things did not end there. Near the end of 1938, under the Imredy government, a "second Jewish law" was crafted and then passed by the Teleki government despite the new prime minister's strong anti-Nazi and anti-fascist sentiments. This second law was much more oppressive, but still did not use a strictly racial definition for Jews. The children of two Jewish parents who had converted were not counted, along with decorated and wounded veterans, and Olympic champions. This law set further restrictions, forced Jews entirely out of certain professions, and set restrictions of Jews' ability to buy and sell land. Again, there was strong opposition, from the left,

---

[128] Hanebrink, 138-139; Mendelsohn, 116-117.

from Jews in parliament, and from many conservative elites, including Bethlen, who was among those who wrote Horthy to voice their opposition. However, Bethlen did believe that the Jewish issue had to be resolved soon due to both foreign and international fascist pressure. He did not attack the law from a moral stance, but rather from an economic one, voicing concern of how this would impact the nation's economy. Unfortunately, as we lack writings by Bethlen we cannot say for certain if this is what he believed or if he was using the arguments he thought would be most likely to persuade Horthy to intervene. Based on what we do know, the latter is more likely. It is clear that the Hungarian establishment was bending in response to pressure from the far right both within and without, and as Mendelsohn puts it, "the old ruling class had become the captive, whether willingly or not, and for whatever reason, to the radical anti-Semitism of the extreme right." In the case of many who identified as part of the conservative, establishment elites, such as Bethlen, it was decidedly unwilling, with Bethlen personally arguing against the law, making use of economic arguments rather than moral ones. While it can be argued that Bethlen did so because he did not particularly care for the Jews and simply thought the law would lead to economic problems, his history makes it more likely that in this instance he made use of pragmatic arguments more likely to sway precisely those people who, while not adherents to the radical right, did not particularly care for Hungary's Jews.[129]

However, the impact was not particularly severe, at least not right away. The regulations were very ineffectually enforced, and things continued largely as usual, to the chagrin of local and foreign fascists. Mendelsohn writes that while the Jewish elite was largely undamaged, many lower class Jews were hard hit, losing their jobs and being unable to find new ones, though again the severity varied depending on who was enforcing the laws. That said, it was another step down a dark path, and in 1939 the question was raised if Jews were worthy to serve alongside Christian Hungarians in the military as enlisted men, a problem which was solved by the creation of unarmed "labor

---

[129] Mendelsohn, 118-122.

battalions," which were not originally for Jews alone, but eventually became so. Another change due to these laws came from within the Jewish community itself. The establishment leadership, despite becoming more vocal, maintained its longtime stance of promoting Magyar patriotism within the Jewish community, maintaining its Hungarian identity, and going along with the regime. Many Jews, however, finally began to embrace Jewish nationalism and Zionism, some emigrated, and others converted. This was helped by the addition of Jews from the recently reclaimed territories, who were more open to Zionism, though the vast majority remained as they had throughout the interwar period.[130]

While the Jewish community sought to maintain the status quo, the growing far right also sought to bring about change. Citing the failure of Hungary to secure territorial revision peacefully, it saw Germany as the answer to the problem. Szalasi's speeches and views may have often been incoherent, but his followers heard the things they wanted to hear. The military played a significant role in the growing popularity of the far right, but Szalasi also played up the religious aspect, citing a need to firm up Hungary's Christian national ideals, using it as a uniting tool, supporting the nationalist goals. These far right Christian nationalists would not refer to each other by their Christian denominations, but as Christian Hungarians—Hungarians first. Hanebrink adds that this idea extended even to prayers, where the "God of the Hungarians (*a magyarok Istene*) was invoked as opposed to normal religious figures like the Virgin Mary. This attempt to put nation above religion did concern some religious leaders, who were aware of the goings-on in Germany in regards to the role of religion. Additionally, some doubted the devotion of the far right to Christianity, as they would celebrate their Christianity in different ways than the conservative establishment, such as their preference for St. Laszlo (who had forbidden marriages between Christians and Jews) as opposed to the more mainstream St. Istvan. In response, the conservative establishment, which had been combating the Arrow Cross politically and legally, sought to take advantage of an auspicious

---

[130] Mendelsohn, 122-124.

religious anniversary,[131] organizing an International Eucharistic Congress, with Vatican support. This had always been seen as a way to demonstrate religious opposition to far left politics, but by 1938 fascism was also a concern, and this was mentioned during the congress, which took on an anti-extremist, anti-social upheaval role. The Arrow Cross did attack this idea, but the congress was ultimately undisturbed. This did, however, illustrate further divides within Hungary, in the area of religious leadership. This phenomenon was seen among Hungarian Protestants as well, as populist and antisemitic ideas grew more popular. Here as well, however, there were divisions, with church leaders noting that their churchgoers reacted badly to anti-fascist statements. The general response was to compromise, emphasizing broad church principles and preaching "spiritual-only antisemitism." It was opposition to the growing fascist sentiment, but a weak one, and things slid further rightward.[132]

---

[131] The nine hundredth anniversary of the death of St. Istvan, the Christian king and saint who came to embody a conservative vision of Christian Hungary in the interwar period.

[132] Hanebrink, 140-143, 145-148, 148-154.

CHAPTER 3

Over The Precipice: The Second World War

Several key developments and events that took place in Hungary during Would War II deserve closer analysis, with the aid of available primary sources, including Hungary's actions (or lack thereof) at the start of the war in 1939, its entry into the war in 1941, the events surrounding Hungary's declaration of war on the Soviet Union later that year, the treatment of Hungary's Jews both prior to and during the German occupation in 1944, and Horthy's ultimately failed attempt to pull Hungary out of the war. While this five year period is shorter than, say, the 1920s or 1930s, there is a great deal to discuss. As such, we will tackle these complicated years in several subsections.

Part 1: Teleki's Gambit: Hungary's Attempt to Remain above the Fray

By the time of Imredy's resignation in 1939, it was clear to most that war was coming. The key question for countries like Hungary was what role they would play in it. The appointment of Count Pal Teleki to the position of prime minister in place of Imredy is a good indicator of the leanings of at least the conservative elites at that juncture. Teleki was very much a conservative, both in social matters as well as in his opposition to German hegemony in Europe. He was a staunch nationalist as well as an antisemite (though not remotely in the same sense as fascist antisemitism.) His primary goal was to keep Hungary out of a conflict with the West, though he recognized that completely divorcing from Germany was next to impossible. That being the case, Teleki took steps to stabilize Hungary's position as a "lower level" ally of Germany, as engineered by Imredy and his foreign minister Count Istvan Csaky. Teleki kept the German-friendly Csaky at the foreign ministry, and restated Hungary's loyalty to the Axis Powers in the event of war, though he stated point-blank that Hungary would not take part in any hostilities directed at Poland. Finally, Teleki oversaw the passage of the Second Jewish Law. During his term, the dismemberment of Czechoslovakia was completed, and Hungary regained multiple territories it had lost at Trianon, including Ruthenia and Transylvania. Also, in a secret-ballot election, the far right gained significant power in parliament. When Germany invaded Poland on September 1, 1939, Teleki maintained Hungary's non-belligerent status, and Germany did not press the issue, as Hungary's assistance was not required. The level of support and loyalty Hungary had to Poland, however, far exceeded simple non-belligerence. Hungary took in hundreds of thousands of Polish refugees, including significant numbers of soldiers, who were sheltered or assisted in traveling west to join the Allies, as well as several thousand Jews.[133]

Furthermore, despite Hungary's antipathy toward the Soviet Union, cordial diplomatic relations were soon established with it due to the Soviet alliance with Germany. Hungary was less cordial with its neighbor Romania, and sought additional territorial revision at Romania's expense. Barely days after the war began, Hungary offered Germany passage of its troops through Hungary if Hungary would be granted permission to seize Transylvania from Romania by force. Hitler was not interested, but after the Soviet Union annexed Bessarabia, and following additional Hungarian agitation, Germany granted a portion of Transylvania to Hungary in the Second Vienna Award, though both Hungary and Romania were unsatisfied. The former because it was not enough and left key resources and population as part of Romania, the latter because it seemed Romania was being slowly dismembered. In reaction,

---

[133] Seton-Watson, 195-197; Macartney, 229-320; Deak, 31.

Romania strongly threw itself into the war as a full ally with Germany to gain favor. This led Hungary to sign the Tripartite Pact on November 2, 1940, as a way to show commitment to Germany and prevent a reversal of the Vienna Award. Teleki, simultaneously, attempted to assert Hungary's diplomatic independence by signing a "Pact of Eternal Friendship" with Yugoslavia on December 12, 1940, with an intent to withstand German pressure, though Germany actually supported the move, as it hoped to bring Yugoslavia into the Tripartite Pact, which it did on March 25, 1941. However, mere days later, a group of Yugoslav military officers overthrew the country's regent and government, and Hitler immediately drew up plans to invade Yugoslavia in retaliation for this betrayal, this time with Hungarian assistance in mind. Teleki was in an impossible position. On the one hand, sending troops to Yugoslavia would gain Hungary additional territory that had been lost after the First World War, but doing so would make them active participants in the war, and Great Britain had already threatened to declare war on Hungary if it invaded Yugoslavia. By this time, many elements of the government, including Horthy, who was drawn in by the prospect of territorial revision, and Foreign Minister Laszlo Bardossy, were in favor of participation in principle, with conditions. There were attempts to couch Hungary's involvement in a way that would not have them branded as invaders, such as not mobilizing until after Yugoslavia was broken up, but Teleki saw even this leading to Hungary being fully pulled into the war. On April 2, 1941, German troops were allowed to cross Hungary to assault Yugoslavia, and the British threatened to cut off diplomatic relations immediately. Teleki, in despair at the new developments, committed suicide that night.[134]

Hungary's decisions upon the start of the war in 1939 seem to best represent the attitudes of the conservative establishment, and emphasize the tricky situation in which Hungary found itself. At least while Teleki was prime minister, there is no question that the government attempted to maintain Hungary's independence from German influence, to retain diplomatic ties with the West, and to not betray its previous commitments.

---

[134] Deak, 31-32; Macartney, 230-231; Ormos, 250-251.

However, the thought of territorial revision was still on the minds of everyone in power, Teleki and Horthy included. Horthy in particular had initially been attracted by the Germans because of the possibility of revision, but he maintained his view that attempting to do so in a belligerent manner, and without the consent of the western powers, was foolish. Imredy was replaced precisely because he was giving in too easily to German pressure. If Horthy had been more willing to work with the Germans while Imredy was prime minister, he was certainly less so with Teleki in the position. As Sakmyster writes, Horthy trusted Teleki implicitly and had no fear that he would try and grant himself more power or give in to the demands of Germany or Hungary's far right. And while Horthy did not prevent Teleki, who was more antisemitic than even Horthy, from passing the second anti-Jewish law, Horthy did insert exemptions for Jews who had made important contributions to the country, going so far as to say that those Jews were as Hungarian as he was. Sakmyster adds that Horthy had become more bitter toward the Germans, and when asked by British and American envoys what he would do if Germany provoked a war, he stated that he would keep Hungary neutral as long as he possibly could. And if German troops entered the country, he would fight to the last. Bombastic, overdramatic answers though they might be, they make his intentions, at least as of 1939, quite clear.[135]

In his memoir, Horthy compares the situation at the start of World War II to that of World War I. In regard to the latter, Horthy writes that Austria-Hungary had grounds to declare a defensive war, citing the assassination of Archduke Ferdinand and "Russian conspiracies." Regarding the Second World War, Horthy writes that Hitler's invasion of Poland could in no way be termed defensive, even if the territorial distribution from the Treaty of Versailles was unjust. He also adds that, ironically, Russia, or rather the Soviet Union, was even a greater threat in 1939 than it had been in 1914, but Hitler made a pact with the Soviets in order to invade Poland. Horthy also points out a fascinating difference in perspective between the then neighboring countries. While anger over the loss of the First World War was directed by

---

[135] Sakmyster, 217-223, 228-230; Szucs and Szinai, 103-105..

Hungary at the successor states created by the war, and while it sought to strengthen ties with the Great Powers to obtain territorial revision, Germany directed its anger at the Great Powers. Horthy also states that the National Socialist philosophy was "repugnant" to him, a feeling enhanced by its influence on Hungarian politics—though it is entirely likely that its threatening of the status quo in Hungary was the more pressing issue for him.[136]

It was Hungary's actions during the German invasion of Poland, however, that makes the greatest case for the Horthy regime's goal of non-belligerence and old-world sense of honor. As mentioned above, Hungary not only remained neutral during the invasion, but openly took in hundreds of thousands of refugees, including Polish military personnel and Jews. In his memoir, Horthy is very explicit when he states that he would not permit Hungary to have any part in an attack on Poland, which he earlier described as having an ancient tradition of friendship with Hungary. He also adds that he unequivocally refused to allow German troops to use railroads under Hungary's control, and gave orders to blow up bridges should the Germans attempt to cross them. He then interestingly describes the general mood of Hungary at the time of the invasion of Poland as being largely in support of neutrality, and that there was a general change of mood as the Germans blitzkrieg had incredible early success. John Flournoy Montgomery, who at that time was still serving as the American minister in Hungary, adds some details to the story of Hungarian-Polish friendship. He notes that many of the Polish soldiers Hungary allowed to enter and who then joined the Allies played an important role in the Battle of Britain, and that in Hungary the Poles were warmly welcomed and Polish-language schools were even established. Horthy's daughter in law, Ilona Edelsheim Gyulai (later Bowden), whose memoir will be discussed in more detail later on, makes a fascinating point in her book in regard to the Poland situation. Had Hungary not sought, and obtained, territory through the German dismemberment of Czechoslovakia in 1938, it would not have shared a border with Poland, and

---

[136] Horthy, 205-207.

there would have been nowhere for refugees to go. It is highly unlikely that this was intentional, as Horthy expressed gratitude to the Germans after recovering the territory, but that does not take away from Hungary's admirable actions in 1939 regarding Poland.[137]

Less uplifting is how Hungary handled the situation in Yugoslavia—with which it had recently signed a Treaty of Eternal Friendship—in 1941. In fact, its main adversary at that point was Romania, which was also part of the Tripartite Pact, but was it ultimately against Yugoslavia that Hungary took action.[138] After the coup in Yugoslavia, and its withdrawal from the Tripartite Pact, Hitler planned to invade, and this time Hungary took part. Unlike before, Germany actively demanded Hungarian cooperation. Beyond that, Hungary's pro-German general staff of the army had been in communication with its German counterpart, without informing Horthy, Teleki, or Parliament. Once again, the radicalized military demonstrated a departure in approach from the conservative establishment. Furthermore, the military made preparations for action and put continual pressure on the government. Added to the unexpected success of the German blitzkrieg, this pro-German attitude led public support for Germany to skyrocket. Despite efforts by Teleki to positively greet the recovery of territory, his pro-western view was widely discredited, and many influential Hungarians urged Horthy to replace Teleki and completely commit to support Germany in all aspects. Horthy, however, refused, and even prevented Teleki from resigning on his own. Teleki served to counterbalance advice from General Werth, who was taking every opportunity to persuade Horthy to strongly support the Germans. Later, in 1940, when Hungary and Romania nearly came to blows and the military pushed for armed action, Teleki and Horthy resisted the pressure and accepted German arbitration on the issue. However, Teleki began to feel more

---

[137] Horthy, 211-213; John Flournoy Montgomery, *Hungary: The Unwilling Satellite* (Morristown, NJ: Vista Books, 1993), 107, 123-124; Bowden, 23; Sakmyster, 230-232.
[138] Of primary concern to Hungary was the region of Transylvania, and it regained control of northern Transylvania (about half of the territory, through the Second Vienna Award in 1940.

and more that Hungary had two governments, the official one and a separate military one.[139]

Eventually, however, as German plans for invading Yugoslavia were drawn up, the prospects for Teleki grew worse and Horthy began to bend under internal pressure and enticing German offers. In particular, he was drawn to the possibility of not just regaining lost territories from Yugoslavia, but also of obtaining from it a port on the Adriatic Sea. Horthy, Sakmyster writes, had reacted emotionally and began to believe that Hungary would look weak if it did not move to take advantage, though Teleki argued that if it took part in the attack they would "lose face before the whole world."[140] Horthy also argued that though Hungary had signed a treaty with Yugoslavia, the coup meant that the people they had signed the treaty with were no longer in power. Eventually, Horthy agreed to moderate his decision, and while he sent a positive response to Hitler, he did not officially commit to military assistance. As Sakmyster puts it, his initial impulsive feelings faded and he decided that Hungary would only liberate Magyars, and would act only after Yugoslavia as a state ceased to exist. As mentioned above, once he learned that the British would cut ties with Hungary if it participated, and that German troops were passing through in order to attack, Teleki committed suicide. In his suicide note, Teleki implied that Horthy shared at least some blame for his death. But Horthy did not get the hint and proceeded with the plan. He said as much to the British envoy, adding that as Hungary could not expect British support, he had to work with Germany, to do at least the minimum to avoid angering the much more powerful country. He still resisted a wholehearted alliance with Germany, despite the wishes of the military chiefs.[141]

In his memoir, Horthy downplays his initial enthusiasm for Hitler's offer of territory, and appears to describe the events from the point where he had

[139] Sakmyster, 248-250; Stephen D. Kertesz, *Diplomacy in a Whirlpool: Hungary Between Nazi Germany and Soviet Russia* (Notre Dame, IN: University of Notre Dame Press, 1953), 52-53.
[140] Sakmyster, 256.
[141] Sakmyster, 256-261; Kertesz, 52-54.

let that subside. He discusses trying to stay non-belligerent out of the belief that Germany would ultimately lose the war, but also out of recognition of Hungary's difficult position. Outright refusal to assist Germany again could lead to an invasion of Hungary, and they could not rely on the west or on a government in exile. He feels Teleki ended his life to avoid giving his approval to the invasion of Yugoslavia, which would lead to war with Great Britain. The memoir of Horthy's daughter-in-law adds another perspective on the situation. She writes that Horthy was in agreement with Teleki about avoiding an active role in the war and pursuing revision peacefully. She also cites a Hungarian military officer who noted the tension between the military and civilian government, as well as historian Peter Gostonyi, who argues that Hungary had no choice but to at least allow German forces passage through the country or risk a war that it was neither capable or willing to fight—it is hard to picture the largely pro-German military fighting the Germans. Bowden also highlights the role that her husband, Horthy's son Istvan, played, something that the secondary sources do not touch on. According to Bowden, Istvan worked hard to bring the activities of the pro-German generals to Horthy's attention and argued for their removal. Bowden also writes that she spoke with Horthy herself, and he said to her that he believed refusing Hitler would lead to an invasion of Hungary. American minister John Flournoy Montgomery also writes that while fault can be found in Hungary's participation, it was by that point swept up in the war, despite a dislike for the Axis. He cites Horthy's pleasure at Italy's troubles in Greece, as it set back the Axis agenda.[142]

Part 2: Hungary at War

With Hungary's situation complicated enough before Teleki's suicide, Horthy hurriedly appointed the arguably unqualified Laszlo Bardossy as prime minister. Despite the shock of Teleki's suicide and the threats by the

---

[142] Horthy, 220-223; Szucs and Szinai, 174-177; Bowden, 68-70, Montgomery, 146-149.

western powers, Hungary emerged unscathed from the Yugoslavia event, as the western threats were not carried out, a development which some historians attribute to Teleki's suicide. However, as Teleki had feared, Hungary was soon pulled further in. On June 22, 1941, Nazi Germany invaded the Soviet Union, and its allies Romania and Finland declared war as well. Initially, Hitler did not ask for Hungarian participation, and attempts by the far right general staff of the Hungarian military to have the Germans put pressure on Hungary to participate failed, though Germany welcomed voluntary support. Prior to the German attack, the Chief of the General Staff, General Henrik Werth tried and failed to convince Horthy to grant permission for the army to take part, despite claiming that doing so would greatly further the goal of territorial revision. Horthy appeared to be siding with those of Teleki's mindset, who believed Germany would lose the war, and that Hungary should remain as non-belligerent as possible so as to stay in the good graces of the Allies. Everything changed, however, on June 26, when there was a small air raid on the town of Kassa (Kosice). This was a gift for those in favor of war, and Bardossy and other jumped on it immediately. When presented with what appeared to be conclusive evidence of an unprovoked Soviet attack on Hungary, Horthy angrily ordered war declared, as well as reprisal attacks. Later that day, the cabinet adopted a similar motion. Parliament never voted on the issue.[143]

To this day, the truth of the bombing of Kassa remains foggy, with no conclusive evidence to support any of the several theories posited.[144] Whatever the case, whether the attack was of Soviet or other origin, Hungary was presented with a *casus belli,* and as of June 26, 1941, Hungary was at war with the Soviet Union, now a full-fledged participant in the Second World War.[145]

Shortly thereafter, Hungary sent its first forces to the Soviet front, an army of approximately 40,000 men. Hungary, however, held off sending more troops until German pressure forced it to commit another 200,000. The

---

[143] Romsics, 204-205; Ormos, 253; Deak, 33; Dreisziger, 175-177
[144] Other possibilities include the bombings having been done in error by Soviet planes, or by Czech or Slovak pilots fleeing toward the Soviet Union.
[145] Deak, 33; Dreisziger, 167-175.

government, or at least Horthy and his conservative associates quickly had second thoughts about taking part in the war. By December of that year, Hungary was also at war with Great Britain and the United States. Britain recognized the Czechoslovak government in exile and withdrew its recognition of the First Vienna Award. By early 1942, the rift between Horthy and Bardossy, as well as that between Horthy and elements of the military, grew wider. Horthy dismissed the strongly pro-German General Werth, and his replacement, General Ferenc Szombathelyi, oversaw the withdrawal of some of the troops sent to the front. By March of that year, Horthy replaced Bardossy as well. The prime minister had become too subservient to the Germans, and there were strong elements in both the government and society that were displeased about the pro-German and pro-war attitude of the Bardossy administration. Additionally, under the Bardossy government life for Hungary's Jews further deteriorated with the passing of the Third Anti-Jewish Law, which was the first to racially define Jews in line with the Nuremburg laws. Additionally, 15,000 non-citizen Jews were deported from Hungary to a region in Ukraine under Hungarian control, which would later fall under German control. Most were massacred by German *Einsatzgruppen*, with some Hungarian military help. Additionally, around the same time, we have arguably the most infamous incident involving Hungary's army during the war, the massacre at Ujvidek (Novi Sad). In this incident, approximately 5,000 Jews and Serbs were killed by Hungarian soldiers and gendarmes in reprisal for partisan activity.[146]

We cannot pass over discussion of Hungary's participation in the occupation of Yugoslavia without addressing the Ujvidek massacre of January 1942. Among the anti-German politicians in parliament, there was a call for investigation and Horthy was given a long memorandum with details on the crimes committed. However, in this case Horthy's military upbringing seemed to prevail, and he was loathe to believe the charges leveled at the officers involved, taking the testimony of the ranking officer on scene at face value. This reaction is reminiscent of Horthy's reaction to the killings during

---

[146] Deak, 35-36; Macartney, 232-233; Ormos, 254-255; Romsics, 205-209.

the White Terror, when he did not acknowledge the crimes of military officers out of a sense of camaraderie and faith in an officer's honor. Later that year, after Miklos Kallay replaced Bardossy as prime minister, Horthy agreed to an investigation. This was done at Kallay's behest, to preserve Hungary's "traditional standards of honor and humanity."[147] Unfortunately, this first investigation amounted to nothing, as the officer in charge was secretly an Arrow Cross member, and the accused were exonerated. In late 1942 and early 1943, however, after further urging by anti-German members of the government, another investigation was conducted. This time there were court martials against over two dozen officers. However, the most important defendants escaped to Germany with German assistance before the proceedings could conclude, and the occupation in 1944 put an end to the ongoing cases.[148]

In his memoir, Horthy does not mention the Ujvidek incident. Why he does not discuss it is a matter of speculation; it is entirely possible he simply did not want to discuss a difficult incident in which, while he was not personally involved—he certainly did not give an order that led to the massacre—his unwillingness to act to crack down on the perpetrators does not help his image. However, he has his defenders. Bowden, who describes herself as having been very distressed at the news, writes in her memoir that the incident was covered up by the pro-Nazi officers involved. Both Horthy and Bardossy were misled about the details, and information was late to reach them. She writes that when Horthy was finally informed of the truth of the matter, he quickly ordered an investigation. Miklos Kallay, who was prime minister during the primary investigation, similarly states that Horthy was grossly misinformed about the incident, and that once he was properly informed quickly agreed to court-martial the perpetrators. In both of these accounts, the blame is placed squarely on the pro-German military. In some respects, this matches what most secondary sources say, apart from laying blame on Horthy. It of course is also relevant that both Bowden and Kallay were closer to Horthy, and would have reason to portray him in a better light.

---

[147] Sakmyster, 288.
[148] Kertesz, 57-58; Sakmyster, 287-288.

But as far as accuracy is concerned, Bowden's account in particular deserves consideration because the diaries she kept during this time served as basis for her memoir, meaning that what she writes is almost certainly what she knew or believed at the time.[149]

What is clear from this incident is that the divide between the Hungarian civilian government and the military was growing wider and wider, with the military imitating Nazi tactics, hiding the truth from the more moderate civilian government, and when all else failed, outright using German connections to help fellow conspirators escape. Horthy did begin to take steps to rectify this problem, such as when he replaced the pliant Bardossy with the more loyal Kally, and when he dismissed General Werth, but he remained too trusting of his underlings.

We see a similar phenomenon play out in regard to Hungary's declaration of war on the Soviet Union on June 27, 1941. Five days earlier, the Germans had begun their invasion, and in the days leading up to it, the general staff, which was at least generally aware of the German plan, had been pushing Horthy to commit to fighting alongside the Germans. Just before the attack was launched, Horthy received a letter from Hitler containing an "explanation" for the invasion and thanking Hungary for taking defensive precautions. But it did not request Hungarian participation. Horthy is described as having reacted with great joy at the news that the crusade against Bolshevism that he had championed earlier in his time as regent was finally beginning—but at the same time, he made no move to involve Hungary, and even seemed to actively avoid over the next few days German officials who might be brining requests of assistance. Sakmyster writes that when Werth and Minister of Defense Karoly Bartha, both of whom were pro-German, sought to convince Horthy to sanction action, they had to travel to his home in Kenderes to meet with him.[150]

---

[149] Miklos Kallay, *Hungarian Premier: A Personal Account of a Nation's Struggle in the Second World War* (New York: Columbia University Press, 1954), 107-110; Bowden, 78, 81-82.

[150] Mario Fenyo, *Hitler, Horthy, and Hungary: German-Hungarian Relations, 1941-1944.* (New Haven and London: Yale University Press, 1972), 15-16; Sakmyster, 265-266.

At the meeting, Werth and Bartha put forward several arguments as to why Hungary should get involved, but Horthy was not swayed, stating that he failed to see any realistic gain for Hungary. At the conclusion of the meeting, Werth and Bartha, perhaps as a veiled threat, stated that the pro-war feeling was so strong in the military that continued inaction could prompt a military coup. Whether or not that would have actually happened is pure speculation, but the fact that two high ranking men raised the possibility at all speaks volumes about the situation in mid-1941. The rest of the civilian government sided with Horthy, though it made the concession of severing diplomatic relations with the Soviet Union on June 23. Then, three days later, the pro-war elements had a stroke of luck—or took matters into their own hands, depending on one's analysis of the bombing of Kassa. The bombing itself was a relatively simple affair. On the morning of the 26th, presumably Russian planes had bombed the small town as well as a nearby railway, killing twenty-six civilians. When informed of this, Horthy was outraged at the apparently unprovoked attack, and after conferring with Bardossy decided that retaliation was warranted, and war was declared the next day. Horthy, despite his earlier reluctance to get Hungary involved in the war, has been described as enthusiastic and happy to be able to take part in the war on communism, and as recently as two months earlier Horthy had written Hitler about the "bolshevist peril." However, things are not so simple. There is some evidence that Horthy expected that Bardossy would discuss the matter with the cabinet, then report back to Horthy before taking action. Instead, after the cabinet meeting Bardossy, assuming he had Horthy's support, declared war without consulting Horthy again, and without consulting Parliament.[151]

However, the questions surrounding the bombing of Kassa and Hungary's subsequent declaration of war do not end there. While the official report blamed the bombing on the Soviets, the possibility that the bombing was a plot orchestrated by the Germans and pro-German Hungarian military personnel to force Hungary into the war has never been conclusively disproven. Evidence to support that theory included at least one eyewitness

---

[151] Sakmyster, 265-267; Szucs and Szinai, 179-183.

on the ground, who was ordered to remain silent. Additionally, there remains the question of *why* the Soviets would risk Hungary entering the war in exchange for the minimal damage the bombing raid inflicted. Furthermore, shortly after the attack, Hungary's minister in Moscow relayed a letter from Vyacheslav Molotov, the Soviet foreign minister, in which Molotov stated that they had not been behind the bombing. Horthy did not see this letter until some time later, as it was concealed from him by the increasingly pro-German Bardossy. In his memoir, Horthy makes a point of this, stating that with the letter from Moscow concealed, he had been presented with a *fait accompli*, and writing in the 1950s, seems to believe whole-heartedly that the Hungarian military was behind the attack to force a confrontation with the USSR; Horthy also mentions other reasons that made a Soviet attack less likely, such as the weakness of their air force as they were falling back in the face of the German blitzkrieg. However, it is impossible to tell if this is what he truly thought during the war, or if this was an after the fact rationalization, either after the war or once his enthusiasm for the war subsided near the end of 1941.[152]

Bowden gives some support to Horthy's words, however, as she mentions specifically remembering his anger upon learning about the concealed letter in 1944, and mentions Bardossy's continuing shift toward Germany. While this testimony, which is not cited in any available secondary sources, is certainly not enough evidence on its own to conclusively prove Horthy's sincerity in his memoir, Bowden's proximity to Horthy, plus the fact that she was writing based on her diaries, lends significant support to this possibility.[153]

Over the next several months, Hungary's not especially powerful army participated in the invasion of the Soviet Union alongside the Germans; it did not make much of an impression on its German counterpart.[154] Within a month of the campaign's beginning General Werth was already pushing for an increased military commitment. As we touched on above, Werth soon

---

[152] Sakmyster, 266-267; Horthy, 230-231.
[153] Bowden, 71-73.
[154] They were ill-equipped, not as well trained as the German forces, and did not perform particularly well in the field.

clashed with Bardossy not over policy, but over Werth's inserting himself into areas that were the prerogative of the prime minister and regent. Faced with a choice between prime minister or chief of staff, Horthy dismissed Werth. It would seem that after only a month Horthy and his administration were regretting entering the war, a decision which was to place them at odds with Great Britain, which Horthy still believed would win thanks to its strong navy. He began to seek ways to limit Hungary's participation and pull forces out. The Germans declined the request, and to make matters worse, in December, after Great Britain declared war on Hungary, Bardossy declared Hungary to be at war with the Unites States without consulting Horthy, the cabinet, or parliament—all while Horthy was ill at home, with rumors abounding that he was possibly dying. Thus, Horthy returned to Budapest to find the country in a lamentable situation, Sakmyster emphasizes Horthy's frustration by citing Horthy's words to the American diplomat Howard Travers, prior to the latter's departure: "Remember that this so-called declaration of war is not legal, was not approved by Parliament, not signed by me."[155]

It is important to note that by this point in the war, despite the stalling of the German advance into Russia, the Axis seemed on course to win the war. A common explanation given by Horthy critics for some of his actions later in the war was that he was trying to make himself look better so as to avoid criminal charges after the war. However, the fact that in many respects he held similar attitudes even when Germany was winning would seem to make that less likely. The Germans, well aware of Horthy's recalcitrance, agreed to let Hungary's deployed forces withdraw, on the condition that more, fresh troops be deployed. Additionally, the new chief of staff, Ferenc Szombathelyi, was of German descent and at least believed by the Germans to be favorably disposed toward their cause. By early 1942, the growing dislike of the Germans within at least the ruling class in Hungary was noticeable to Italy's foreign minister count Ciano, who, in a January 1942 visit to Budapest, wrote that every Hungarian he met had something bad to say about the Germans.[156]

---

[155] Sakmyster, 270-274.
[156] Fenyo, 30-38.

Part 3: Family Matters: Horthy's Anti-Nazi Son

Another significant event in 1942 was the appointment of Horthy's oldest son Istvan to the position of deputy regent. While he tragically died that same year, he is important in that he was someone Horthy confided in and trusted. He was also Horthy's planned successor. He is discussed somewhat in secondary sources, but Bowden, to whom he was married for over two years, devotes significant attention to him in her memoir, and through understanding him and his position we can better understand Horthy. Whereas Horthy was very much a man of the old world, Istvan belonged to the new one, though he never bought into the radical politics that were a hallmark of interwar Europe. Istvan also acted unlike the son of the head of state and was very much his own man. He led a fascinating life, and his experiences shed light on his convictions. He became a member of Hungary's Air Force Reserve in 1929, then obtained an engineering degree and worked in a Hungarian factory making aircraft engines, notably refusing any special treatment that his status as the regent's son could have commanded. Several years later, Istvan decided to travel to the United States, where he worked in a Ford factory for eighteen months. Again, he declined any special treatment, and worked his way up to become an engineer in Ford's experimental design division, where he patented at least one car part design and became friendly with Henry Ford. Upon his return to Hungary, Istvan worked at MAVAG, the country's royal railroad production company, eventually becoming its deputy director, and later, director of the State Railways (MAV).[157]

Istvan Horthy's background is relevant to two of the most significant events to happen between Hungary's entry into the war and the German occupation in 1944: Istvan's appointment as deputy regent in February 1942 and his death just over half a year later. Miklos Horthy had long been criticized for his choice to appoint his son as deputy regent, which made Istvan his successor, at least in an interim sense, if he should die in office. Even at the time there was criticism of Horthy, with people alleging he was

---

[157] Bowden, 29-31; Kallay, 16; Sakmyster, 154.

trying to build a dynasty. This is something Horthy vehemently denies in his memoir, stating that he simply believed Istvan to be an ideal candidate for a job that at the moment was only a theoretical and temporary one, as the position of deputy regent was to be dissolved if the deputy were to take up the mantle of regent until a new one was chosen. There is certainly some truth to Horthy's stated reasons, but that was unlikely his only consideration. Certainly, he had at some point contemplated a dynasty of sorts, though to his credit he was consistent in his assertion that he not be crowned king or given any royal title. More likely, he nominated his son because he wanted a deputy who he knew he could trust to be both loyal to him and to not compromise his own ideals. This is where Istvan's experiences and values come into play. Istvan was well traveled and, having spent over a year and a half in the United States, was exposed to modern American culture and ideas. As such, Istvan was well known to be pro-western and very anti-Nazi. He was also known for having close relationships with many influential Jews, to the point that he was branded a "Jew-lover" by Hungary's far right. Additionally, Istvan's experience doing blue-collar work gave him a perspective on the world that his father lacked. Even prior to Istvan's appointment as deputy regent, he had his father's ear, and played a significant role in the dismissal of General Werth. Sakmyster adds that it would have been nearly impossible for Horthy to appoint anyone else so pro-western and anti-Nazi to the position and that, while likely not Horthy's full design, meshed well with his attempts to stack the government with more pro-western elements.[158]

Miklos Kallay, who was a friend of the Horthy family and who was himself appointed prime minister a month after Istvan's appointment, held Istvan in high regard as well. He wrote that, had Istvan lived, the only political difference they would have had is that Istvan would feel Kallay, who was anti-Nazi himself, was not as strongly so as the young deputy regent. He also mentions that during the war Istvan, as well as his wife, Ilona, were very involved in the refugee assistance program. Istvan's wife writes further of his virtues, including his humility and his concern for those working under him,

---

[158] Sakmyster, 171, 271-271, 279; Horthy, 237-240.

both traits he likely acquired and honed during his time as a simple worker.[159]

Istvan's death during a training flight on August 20, 1942, while deployed near the front with his reserve unit, came as a great shock to those who knew him. The death of his oldest son hit Horthy hard. While it is impossible to quantify the emotional toll it took, we can certainly say that with Istvan's death, Horthy—and Hungary—lost a very strong, principled, and influential person at a time when he was most needed. We will discuss the events of 1944 later, but it is safe to say that had Istvan lived, things would certainly have played out differently after the German occupation of Hungary. Additionally, the death of Istvan Horthy is the event that has the most amount of conspiracy theory surrounding it apart from the bombing of Kassa. The circumstances of Istvan's death seem straightforward; during a training flight, as he tried to rapidly ascend, his plane stalled and crashed. However, both Horthy and Istvan's wife, Ilona, bring up the possibility that his death was no accident, and certainly not due to Istvan being drunk—a rumor allegedly propagated by Nazi and Arrow Cross men. Istvan's anti-Nazi and pro-Jewish feelings were public knowledge, and Nazi Germany had made its feelings toward him clear when they did not send representatives to congratulate him on his appointment as deputy regent. Furthermore, Istvan's fatal flight was to have been his last before returning to Budapest to engage more actively in government matters alongside his father. In her memoir, Bowden also tells of a secret conversation she had with her husband shortly before his death, while staying in a villa at the invitation of a German officer in Kiev, where she was visiting Istvan. He had detailed a plan to fly to Great Britain or the United States, as he felt he could do more to help Hungary from there. He believed that Hungary had far too many people, especially in military positions, who believed in a German victory, and was even willing to be denounced as a traitor so as to not have his family connected with his plans. Bowden states that she later learned that the house had been bugged, and wonders why neither she nor Istvan, who had always been careful to consider such things, had not thought to worry about that.[160]

---

[159] Kallay, 16, 334; Bowden, 30-34.
[160] Bowden, 104-105, 155-128; Sakmyster, 298-299; Kallay, 104-105.

Of course, there is no way to say with certainty that Istvan Horthy was murdered, but it cannot be ruled out; furthermore, most of the details provided by Bowden have not been taken into account by most secondary sources. What we can take from the story of Istvan Horthy's appointment to the position of deputy regent, and from the questions surrounding his untimely death—not the first among relatives of the leaders of nations allied to Nazi Germany[161]—is that Miklos Horthy was certainly aware that many of the officials, particularly military ones, who surrounded him, could not be relied on. One of the few people he truly trusted was his own son, who was known as pro-western, pro-Jewish, and anti-Nazi. In light of this, it further demonstrates both that Horthy was not simply a "Hitler ally" as some portray him, and that Horthy, as the head of Hungary's civilian government, was increasingly at odds with the more radical elements in the country.

Part 4: Horthy, Prime Minister Kallay, and the Jewish Question

Bardossy was replaced by Miklos Kallay, a conservative statesman whose views closely aligned with those of Bethlen and Horthy. Kallay attempted to make the best of the situation, and started putting out feelers to the West while continuing to fight against the Soviet Union, as he also strongly opposed Bolshevism. However, he had to carefully balance his actions, as he could not risk open conflict with the Germans and possible occupation of Hungary. As a result, under his administration, a fourth anti-Jewish law was passed, as well as a decree calling up Jewish men for labor service with the military, many of whom died due to both battle and cruel treatment by military officers. Additionally, at this point Hungary finally started to suppress left wing and anti-German activities. However, in a crucial area, Kallay's government stubbornly resisted German pressure, that being the Jewish issue, refusing to mark Jews with yellow stars, send them to ghettos, or deport them to camps.

---

[161] Italian dictator Benito Mussolini's son, Bruno, also in his country's air force, also died in a non-combat crash, in 1941.

By spring of 1943, things grew more tense. Hitler had grown impatient with Hungary's unwillingness to comply on the Jewish issue, and a meeting between him and Horthy at Klessheim devolved into a shouting match. In addition, by that time the Soviets had won the Battle of Stalingrad, and the Second Hungarian Army was almost completely wiped out. The primary goal of the Kallay government, therefore, was to find a way out of the war that would not end in Hungary occupied by the Germans or Soviets. To that end, a secret agreement was forged with the British, which stated that Hungary would surrender to western forces. During this time, Hungary began to address the crimes committed by its forces, held back fascist forces within the country, and continued to accept refugees. At this time, Hungary acted nearly like a neutral country. Allied bombers flying over Hungary were not fired upon, nor did they drop bombs, and ties were made to partisan groups as well.[162]

Things took a turn for the worse, however, as Allied plans changed and the western powers no longer planned to send forces to central and eastern Europe, leaving it to the Soviets. Additionally, the Germans were well aware of Hungary's attempts to leave the war, and Hitler decided enough was enough. When Horthy was next at Klessheim and unable to communicate with his counselors at home, Hitler invaded and swiftly occupied the country on March 19, 1944, facing little resistance from the leaderless military. Kallay fled to the Turkish legation, and Hitler appointed his plenipotentiary, Edmund Vessenmayer, to oversee occupied Hungary, and Horthy was compelled to replace Kallay with the pro-German General Dome Sztojay, and appoint Nazi sympathizers to cabinet positions. While Horthy nominally remained in power as regent, he no longer truly controlled Hungary. For the next three months, Horthy took little active role in politics, including with respect to the Jewish issue. As a result, during this time, Adolf Eichmann organized, along with the willing participation of Hungarian gendarmes, Deputy Minister of the Interior Laszlo Endre, and under-secretary Laszlo Baky, the deportation of 434,000 Jews from Hungary. Of this number,

---

[162] Ormos, 257-259; Deak, 36-37; Macartney, 233.

approximately 120,000 survived. There was little organized resistance, as the Gestapo and its Hungarian collaborators arrested anyone they felt could take a leadership role in a resistance movement. Those who escaped capture were forced into hiding. Hungary soon started coming under attack from Allied bombers, and foreign leaders began to lobby Horthy to halt the deportations. All while the Eastern Front drew closer. In later July, Horthy finally threw himself back into the political scene, and had the deportations halted before the Jews of Budapest could be taken—marking the only time a country's leader did such a thing. Additionally, following Romania's switch to the side of the Allies on August 23, Horthy removed key Nazi sympathizers from government, including Baky, Endre, and Sztojay, and appointed the loyal General Geza Lakatos prime minister.[163]

Part 5: The Holocaust in Hungary

By far the most discussed topic relating to the Horthy era during the later war years, and arguably the most important, is the rise of the radical right and the fate of Hungary's Jews. We have already discussed this issue in part, during the interwar years up until the start of the war. But the situation from 1941 onward was extremely complex and its multiple facets intertwined with both the Horthy administration and Hungary's rising far right movements. However, despite the new laws defining Jews racially, Hungary was undoubtedly one of the best places in Nazi-dominated Europe for Jews at the time, especially taking into consideration just how many Jews were in Hungary (over 800,000). Apart from the Ujvidek incident (which occurred in a war zone) and the anti-Jewish laws (none of which was strictly enforced), the only government sanctioned attack on the Jews during this period in Hungary occurred in 1941. After a government ordered internment of non-citizen Jews, one General Jozsef Heszlenyi requested German permission to deport some 15,000 Jews into German-controlled Ukraine. In January 1942, this request was granted, and the deported Jews were quickly massacred by

---

[163] Macartney, 233-234; Deak, 37-38; Ormos, 261-264; Romsics, 209-211.

German forces. This was the only incident where Jews were deported from Hungary prior to the German occupation. While it is known that the interment of the non-citizen Jews was sanctioned by the government, it is unclear if General Heszlenyi carried out the deportation with permission from the Horthy government or if this was purely taken on by antisemitic, pro-German military officials, and unfortunately none of the available primary sources discuss this incident. Given what we have seen regarding the military's attitude, it is not unlikely that this was carried out without the civilian government knowing.[164]

To get a sense of the Horthy administration's general attitude toward Jews leading up to the German occupation, we must, obviously, look deeper into Horthy's personal feelings, as well as those of key people surrounding him, chiefly Miklos Kallay, prime minister starting in March 1942. Horthy, as we have mentioned earlier, was not one who would be termed a "Jew-lover," as his son Istvan was. His relative apathy toward the violence of the White Terror makes that clear, as does his self-description as an antisemite. And, as we have seen, he was perfectly willing to allow the passage of bills restricting the rights of Jews. However, he proved stubbornly resistant to accepting the Nazi style demonization and persecution of Jews. During 1942 and 1943, the Jewish situation hardly changed, and Horthy had a fairly tolerant policy—thus hampering the argument that he only helped Hungary's Jews later on in order to bolster his image as the eventuality of Germany's defeat became clear. In one notable instance, Horthy instructed the director of the Hungarian Radio to avoid dealing with the "Jewish question" in broadcasts, and that it was wrong to think of Jews a monolithic. Incidentally, this fits into the worldview that both Horthy and his longtime trusted associate, Istvan Bethlen, held, that of a class-based view of a person's worth. By this logic, there were of course good Jews who had done great things for the country. And on the other hand, there were of course many that had not, in Horthy's view, and he was certainly less willing to go to bat for them. In another incident, Horthy, along with

---

[164] Fenyo, 69-70; Randolph L. Braham, *Politics of Genocide : The Holocaust in Hungary,* (Detroit: Wayne State University Press, 2000), 56-57; Jeno Levai, ed, *Eichmann in Hungary: Documents* (New York: Howard Fertig, 1987), 48-49.

Kallay, opposed a bill drafted by pro-Nazi finance minister Lajos Remenyi-Schneller which would have done crippling economic damage to Hungary's Jews. While acknowledging the need to limit "Jewish influence," Horthy outright opposed any proposal that amounted to robbery of Hungary's Jews. Kallay was of a similar mind. While he would on occasion make use of antisemitic rhetoric in speeches, and was willing to impose some economic restrictions, he was firmly with Horthy in opposing inhumane measures. When pressed by the Germans or Hungarian Nazis, he would procrastinate working on "extreme measures" until after the war—when Kallay truly hoped to be able to right the limited wrongs already committed.[165]

Horthy and Kallay also took some active measures to assist Hungary's Jews in 1942 after receiving reports of sadistic cruelty on the part of Hungarian military officers. They also took steps to better the situation of the Jews drafted into the army's labor battalions. Horthy later even candidly stated to Hitler and Ribbentrop that he was ashamed to have sent 36,000 Jews to the front in such battalions, where most of them died.[166] His action against this mistreatment is of particular significance because it required him to acknowledge the wrongdoing of military men, something Horthy historically had a very hard time doing, as seen even in the Ujvidek case—though as with Ujvidek, it took time for him to act. Undoubtedly he received hard evidence from sources he trusted. This also gave him another reason to oust the pro-German minister of defense, General Karoly Bartha, and replace him with the loyal and humanitarian General Vilmos Nagy, who attempted to restore discipline and stamp out radicalism among the army officers. Unfortunately, he was not entirely successful, as far-right and pro-German sentiments were so thoroughly embedded in the military, and antisemitic officers would sabotage Nagy's orders. In an ironic twist, Horthy's actions with the labor battalions came just as Germany, through Hungary's representative Dome Sztojay—who was one of few Hungarians who knew the truth about what the deportation of Jews meant—demanded additional actions, including forcing

---

[165] Sakmyster, 147, 286-287.
[166] Horthy had earlier approved of the creation of these battalions, which to him provided Jews, who legally could not join the army, a way to serve.

Jews to wear the yellow star and deportation. Sztojay warned of "fatal consequences" if Hungary did not comply. Horthy refused to do so, in line with his archaic sense of honor. Additionally, by late 1942, it is possible that Horthy and others had pragmatic reasons not to persecute the Jews, based on information passed from the British. To the Germans, Kallay presented several objections, excuses, including economic reasons, a need to know the fate of deported Jews, and the fact that how Hungary dealt with its Jews was an internal matter. In a meeting with Hitler in 1942, Horthy refused to consent to stricter actions against the Jews, and refused to replace Kallay.[167]

In her memoir, Ilona Bowden states very strongly that Horthy strongly resisted pressure to give in to these German demands. She mentions a letter written by Horthy (included in the book *The Confidential Papers of Admiral Horthy*),[168] in which he systematically refutes the charges of being lax on key issues leveled at him and Kallay by the Germans. The extended letter (part of which is also shown in an image in the original German) bears this out.[169]

Horthy and Kallay's refusal to comply on the Jewish issue was one of the primary reasons the Germans decided to occupy Hungary on March 19, 1944. Once the Germans had control of the country, Horthy was pressured into dismissing Kallay and appointing a new, pro-German prime minister, Dome Sztojay. At this point, Horthy made a pair of decisions that remain his most controversial. He first decided not to resign as regent in protest, and then for several months withdrew from active participation in political matters, specifically in regard to the "Jewish question." Of primary importance here is understanding Horthy's reasoning behind his actions, how much he knew about what was going on, and to what extent he approved of

---

[167] Sakmyster, 291-294, 308; Horthy, 248; Kertesz, 75-76; Kallay, 142.

[168] In discussing the book, Bowden is very skeptical of its authenticity, and she does not consider it a reliable historical document. As it was published by Hungary's communist government in 1962, and tries to portray Horthy in a negative light, that it is clearly biased. Additionally, she alleges that she could recognize what her father in law would or would not have written; after the war, she copied and filed each of his letters, and was intimately familiar with his writing and thought style.

[169] Bowden, 137; Szucs and Szinai, 248-257.

the actions. Some historians, like Randolph Braham,[170] portray Horthy in a negative light because of his action—or inaction—at this time.

In his well known book *The Politics of Genocide: The Holocaust in Hungary*, Braham asserts that in choosing to remain in office but withdraw from managing state affairs during the German occupation, Horthy legitimized the occupation, pacified the Hungarian populace, and at least indirectly is responsible for the deportation and murder of over 600,000 Hungarian Jews. Braham argues that Horthy's cooperation with and agreement to supply Germany with "Jewish workers" was key for Germany, as it was preferred to continue to promote the illusion that Hungary was still a sovereign state. Horthy, he writes, was convinced that Germany needed the laborers, and saw this as a chance to rid Hungary of the undesirable "Galician Jews," (though Jews of that status were a minority among those deported.) There is some evidence for this assertion, particularly postwar testimony by Germany's plenipotentiary in Hungary, Edmund Veesenmayer. Additionally, Laszlo Baky, one of the officials chiefly responsible for the mass deportations, believed that Horthy was completely on board based on a previous conversation they had had, where Horthy expressed support for "important" Jews, but seemed willing to be rid of the others, or at least less willing to defy the Germans on their behalf. Others were aware of this latent bias. Later on, when the truth about the deportations began to make its way to Horthy, it was emphasized that Jews Horthy would consider "good," such as war heroes, were being victimized as well as the "other" Jews, such as the Galician Jews in the countryside. Laszlo Endre, the other key officer involved in the deportations, similarly said that Horthy had not objected to the deportations of the "undesirable" Jews, and had said that the sooner it was done the sooner the Germans would leave. However, as Sakmyster points out, there is no record of these conversations aside from Baky and Endre's testimonies at their postwar trials, and as such we must consider the possibility that they made

---

[170] For disclosure's sake, it is relevant to note that Braham, who is Jewish, was born in Transylvania in 1922 and served as a forced laborer in the Hungarian army during the war. As such, he does have a personal connection to this topic which may color his interpretation of the events.

these statements to deflect blame from themselves to Horthy. But Horthy was indisputably aware that deportations did take place, and that the families of the supposed laborers would travel with them. Horthy's statements when discussing the matter make it clear that he believed that scandalous treatment of the Jews ended after his investigation into earlier allegations of cruelty. However, he was also at this time being fed false information by Baky, Endre, and Minister of the Interior Andor Jaross, assuring him that the allegations were mere "gossip of cowardly Jewish sensation-mongers." Sakmyster, while maintaining the argument that Horthy was incapable of imagining that the Germans would simply kill Jews who could be used for labor, writes that he rationalized away the deportation of these "Galician Jews," who he saw as broadly communist, to do forced labor—though he still felt the deportations a distasteful concession to appease Hitler. It is interesting to consider if he would have consented, even begrudgingly, if the upper class Jews he deemed "good" were targeted first, or if he would have consented to allowing poor Magyars to be deported for labor.[171]

What is not in question is that Horthy did not raise objections for approximately three months as he remained withdrawn from government affairs, during which time over 600,000 Jews were deported, nearly all of whom died in Auschwitz. However, assigning blame to Horthy is not quite as simple as looking at his approval, whether active or passive, of the deportations after the occupation. Based on both his writings in his memoir and some of the recorded quotes from him at the time, Horthy, along with many others, was unaware that the Nazis were deporting Hungary's Jews not for labor, but for extermination. Doubtless, Horthy had to have reasoned that being deported for "labor" would hardly be pleasant for the Jews, particularly given what he knew about Hungary's labor battalions. In addition, Horthy had to know that many Hungarian Jews most suitable for labor had already been drafted to the labor battalions. However, there is reason to believe that at this point, with him either believing he had no room to act or choosing not to, that Horthy legitimately believed that deportation for labor was the lesser evil, however distasteful it was

---

[171] Braham, 58-59; Sakmyster, 344-347.

and however hard it would be on the deportees. Something else worth noting is that, during his 1943 meeting with Hitler and other senior Nazi officials at Klessheim, even when they came closest to outright stating their goal of annihilating the Jews, annihilation was presented as an alternative to deportation and camps. Thus, when later Hungary was pressured to enact deportations, it is not unlikely that Horthy rationalized, incorrectly, that Jews being deported meant that they were avoiding extermination. Additionally, Horthy, at least initially, likely bought the lie that the families of the workers were being sent with them for reasons of comfort and latched onto that to rationalize that the Jews were not being sent to their deaths—be it due to harsh conditions and labor or mass extermination.[172]

Horthy also writes that he believed that, if he abdicated, the Arrow Cross would take charge, and exterminate all of Hungary's Jews. The reign of terror the Arrow Cross would wreak on Budapest after Horthy's resignation gives strength to that argument. Later, he states that once he learned the truth regarding the fate of the Jews, he took action, and soon managed to stop the deportations. The main question is whether Horthy truly did not know about the death camps, and if so, when he learned the truth. In his analysis, Braham analyzes the role of Hungary's Jewish leadership, which, in a similar manner to Horthy, chose to retain their positions and attempted to work with the Germans. Based on what information was passed to Hungary's Jewish leadership earlier in the war, plus the arrival of the famous Auschwitz Protocols[173] in 1944, Braham makes it clear that the Jewish leadership at least had an idea of what was really going on. However, this knowledge did not extend to the general Jewish populace, and does not answer the question of how much the Hungarians knew. However, Braham does cite an excerpt from the postwar Veesenmayer trial, where Rudolf Kasztner, a leader of the Zionist

---

[172] Levai, 53-54.

[173] The Auschwitz Protocols, in many instances (including this one) referring specifically to the Vrba-Wetzler Report, was a document compiled by Rudolf Vrba and Alfred Wetzler, two Slovak Jews who escaped from Auschwitz. It was one of, if not the first attempt to estimate the number of people being killed there, and had one of the first detailed descriptions of the gas chambers.

Organization of Hungary, admits that he and other leaders had awareness, but failed to inform Horthy and the Hungarian government.[174]

Braham goes further, however, and alleges that the upper levels of Hungary's government, Horthy included, understood the nature of Germany's war against the Jews. Dome Sztojay, who was Hungary' representative in Germany, and later prime minister after the German occupation, and was aware of the realities of the Holocaust.[175] Additionally, at least one member of the upper house of parliament knew the truth of it too, as did Endre and Baky. However, these are far-right individuals, and it can be reasonably argued that they did not share this knowledge with those who might object. However, Braham admits that the only source for evidence that members of Hungary's more moderate Social Democratic Party were aware of the truth is Kasztner, who did not provide hard evidence for his assertion. Another questionable proof of this by Braham comes from discussing Horthy's meeting with Hitler at Klessheim in 1943. At the meeting, Braham writes, Hitler advised Hungary to shoot Jews who refused to work, and Germany foreign minister Joachim von Ribbentrop said that Jews should be killed or sent to concentration camps. Upon his return, Horthy penned a letter defending himself and Kallay against several accusations Hitler had made, which included Hungary's "weakness" on the Jewish issue. Horthy writes, in an early draft of the letter, that Hungary was accused of not taking as drastic action "in the extirpation of the Jews as Germany had." Braham emphasizes this phrase, which was removed from the final draft, as evidence that Horthy knew the fate of Germany's Jews. However, the word extirpate, which was likely chosen deliberately, specifically describes a situation where a group or species ceases to exist in a specific area, but still exists elsewhere. This does not necessarily mean execution, rather simply removal. And as we will see others argue, there is a strong argument that Horthy simply could not imagine that Germany was exterminating the Jews over which it held power.[176]

---

[174] Braham, 88-94; Kertesz, 80.

[175] Braham, 96.

[176] Braham, 93-95; Szucs and Szinai, 248-255.

Other historians, such as Thomas Sakmyster and Mario Fenyo, see things in a slightly different light. First, in discussing Horthy's choice to remain in office rather than resigning, they give credence to his claim at the time that to abandon his post would mean that he could not do any good at all, and also take into account his old world sense of honor and duty; the captain did not abandon his ship. Despite urging by Kallay and others, Horthy stayed on as regent, aware that he was going to be forced to make numerous concessions to the Germans which would hurt his image. He received other, often conflicting advice at this time as well, such as that of the Jewish establishment urging him to remain in office and appease the Germans by appointing a new government. Istvan Bethlen, however, argued that he should not appoint a new prime minister, not advance the puppet regime at all, to make a statement as well as to make it harder for the Germans to accomplish things. It is also known that the Germans did not want Horthy removed at this time, to make it easier to maintain stability, though they actively sought to separate Horthy from his advisors.[177] They were largely successful, and Horthy was soon without most of his trusted advisors, who were either arrested or in hiding, and he had few people he could rely on close at hand. Under extreme pressure from Veesenmayer and Hitler, Horthy ceased procrastinating and set up a new government, though he put up a bit of a fight regarding ministry appointments.[178]

Was Horthy's decision the correct one? It is difficult to make a firm judgment. On the one hand, historians such as Braham do have a point when they argue that by staying on, Horthy legitimized the occupation, the new government, and what happened to the Jews. A resignation may have also signaled to the people that this was unacceptable, and should be resisted, and it may have made organizing things such as the deportations more difficult. It also would have led to a generally more positive view of Horthy in the future. Additionally, John Montgomery makes the point that the Germans very much sought to maintain at least a veneer of legality, which is why Horthy was presented with an ultimatum rather than assassinated.[179]

---

[177] Levai, 62.
[178] Fenyo, 176-178; Sakmyster, 336-338.
[179] Montgomery, 190-191.

However, the other side of the argument is strong as well, and given the evidence we have discussed, plus taking into account what we know of Horthy, the stronger side. We cannot say for certain that a resignation by Horthy would have done anything positive. Given the high levels of support for the Nazi cause among Hungarians, the military (and gendarmes) in particular, the deportation of Hungary's Jews would likely have taken place in a similar manner, only in this case the Jews of Budapest would have gone as well. We must also take into account the circumstances of the occupation. German troops entered Hungary while Horthy was kept away, unable to give orders. At best, Hungary had a very poor chance of holding off an invasion (even less, due to the ideology of the army officers), and once the Germans were already there, Horthy would have seen it as hopeless. To use a maritime analogy that Horthy would likely have appreciated: he could either abandon ship and make a statement that he was opposed to its takeover but leave its passengers completely at the mercy of the invaders (and mutinous crew members), or remain on and try and effect some good, but recognize that in doing so he would be seen as complicit in what took place on the ship, even though he would no longer be *de jure* in charge. Montgomery also asserts that Horthy in fact took advantage of Hitler's need for legality, and aimed to finally use his extra-constitutional powers.[180]

Sakmyster, in particular, argues that Horthy simply could not comprehend the concept that worker-strapped Germany, which requested Hungary's Jews for "labor," would instead be murdering them. He describes it almost like a psychological break, with Horthy both unwilling and unable to imagine an Auschwitz truly existing, that the families were traveling with the "workers" so they would be more comfortable and not be separated, and he believed that like the thousands of Magyar workers who had been in Germany since the start of the war, they would not be harmed. Another interesting aspect of this coincides with another question and criticism regarding Horthy during this time, namely his withdrawal from all public affairs, including the Jewish issue (which is what the more critical historians

---

[180] Sakmyster, 338-339; Fenyo, 178; Kertesz, 78; Montgomery, 194-195.

emphasize, though Horthy in fact withdrew from all regular activities), for several months after the occupation. The Germans and pro-German Hungarians took advantage of this—and Veesenmayer was even encouraged to isolate Horthy. When the cabinet passed laws, including those pertaining to the Jews, Sztojay would waive the need to seek Horthy's approval, stating that Horthy had given Sztojay a free hand in the matter.[181]

Here we must attempt to understand why Horthy would make this choice, which generally—but not completely—took him out of the daily work of governance for months. Certainly, one likely possibility is that he wanted to dissociate himself with what he knew would be harsh actions against the Jews, though as we have stated it follows that he could not comprehend the true nature of the Final Solution. Only once he received hard evidence could he understand it. Apart from that, he preferred not to dwell on the fate of the Jews—something which, Sakmyster writes, was done by the better informed Jewish leadership as well. Horthy, in private, did also express uneasiness regarding antisemitic propaganda, and in one instance declined an invitation to attend a well known antisemitic play. Beyond dissociating himself, there is another, more psychological reason for his withdrawal. Put simply, Horthy felt overwhelmed, defeated, and helpless, not realizing that he did still have significant influence. But, having been unable to prevent occupation, forced to appoint a government he did not approve of, and cut off from the key conservative advisors he had relied upon for so long, seemingly without support, it is not inconceivable to see him as having been in a state of paralyzed will, unsure both of what should be done and what *could* be done. He had tried, in June, after being informed of the cruel nature of the deportations (but still not of the death camps) to protest inhumane measure which "did not conform to the Hungarian mind," by requesting the dismissal of the notorious Baky and Endre. He also failed to recall Hungary's beleaguered armed forces. To that end, he sent a letter to Hitler via Sztojay, but there were no results. This only added to his feeling of impotence, made him feel more helpless than he was.[182]

---

[181] Sakmyster, 342-343; Fenyo, 178-179.
[182] Fenyo, 178, 201; Sakmyster, 348-349.

Ultimately, it was the arrival of the Auschwitz Protocols through his daughter-in-law Ilona which would give the isolated Horthy a direction in which to move. In the following days, another memorandum, from the Jewish Council, reached Horthy via his son Nicholas, and local and international figures from the pope to the king of Sweden to the president of the United States urged Horthy to stop the deportations—along with threats of additional[183] reprisals. Finally, Horthy acted, and in an unprecedented action in Nazi-occupied Europe, used his authority as head of state to not just halt the deportation of Jews, but even had at least one train en route to Auschwitz turned back. Horthy became revitalized, acting more shrewdly and boldly, taking his opponents by surprise. Sztojay, more loyal to Hitler than to Horthy, nonetheless felt obligated to listen to Horthy, and Veesenmayer, so confident that Horthy was only posturing, and could still be advised to resume deportations soon (if in a less cruel manner) that he told Berlin that everything was under control and reinforcements were not needed. Eichmann, furious, tried to test Horthy's resolve, and was rebuffed. Even though he was under tremendous pressure, and for a time did not replace Sztojay or other pro-German ministers, Horthy did not bend on the Jewish issue. In a speech at a military academy he spoke of righting mistakes and restoring Hungarian honor, and supported numerous initiatives to ease living conditions for the Jews. Additionally, he approved measures to get Jews out, such as a plan (which was never carried out) to have Jews emigrate to neutral countries and the British Mandate of Palestine, and quietly supported the rescue activities of Swedish diplomat Raoul Wallenberg for the rest of his time as regent.[184] Despite further pressure from Germany and from Eichmann directly, Horthy permitted no further deportations and eventually had Eichmann and his men leave Hungary, to Eichmann's fury.[185]

---

[183] Since the start of the German occupation, Hungary had been bombed by the Allies.

[184] Raoul Wallenberg, *Letters and Dispatches, 1924-1944*, trans. Kjersti Board (New York: Arcade Pub., 1995), 240-241, 248-249.

[185] Sakmyster, 352-359; Fenyo, 194-206; Montgomery, 194-196; Kertesz, 79-81; Levai 127-129.

Braham, in his discussion of Horthy's change of attitude, grants Horthy less agency in his decision, emphasizing the many factors that prompted the regent to act when he did (as opposed to earlier, as Braham believes Horthy knew at least most of the truth earlier.) These forces, briefly touched upon above, deserve some analysis before we bring in Bowden's nearly eyewitness account, as well as Kallay's point of view.

Bowden devotes significant attention to the events that took place between the German invasion on March 19, 1944 and the overthrow of the Horthy regime on October 16 of the same year. Early on, she raises a point not addressed by the historians: What would have happened if there had been a vice regent in Hungary while Horthy was unreachable in Germany? This situation was precisely what the office of vice-regent was meant to help with, to have the authority to take major action if the regent was indisposed. Of course, we cannot definitively state that the outcome would have changed, as Hungary would still have been completely outmatched and so many officers and political figures eager to collaborate with the Germans. More importantly, as one of the few people close to Horthy at this time, she gives a good assessment of his state of mind—as well as of her own. She describes Horthy as exhausted and stressed upon his return from Germany, and her account matches Kallay's. Bowden describes herself as being shocked and angry, adding that she had urges to run her car into the German guards outside the palace. In his memoir, Kallay also offers his thoughts on Horthy's decision to stay at his post, despite his own urging that he resign or step back from daily affairs—the latter of which Horthy did. Kallay adds that Horthy's hope to help the whole country and salvage the situation was a lost cause from the start, but at least he was able to help some of Hungary's Jews and spoke for the "true soul and will of the Hungarian people" on October 15, which will we discuss in more detail later.[186]

In discussing Horthy's relative inaction, Bowden writes both that they could only safely accomplish a little at a time without risking the Germans and pro-German Hungarians completely removing Horthy—something that

---

[186] Bowden, 157-158, 161; Kallay, 427-435

was considered—but that while he withdrew from daily affairs he did not become completely apathetic and withdrawn. He simply felt he had little room to act. In regards to the Jewish issue, she writes that through a commission known as the "Escape Office," among other names, she, her brother-in-law Miklos (Nicholas) Horthy Jr., as well as the regent and other anti-Nazi people had been in contact with the Jewish leadership since 1943, helping where they could by granting exemptions for Jews—the office was told that no applicant should be rejected—which helped many Jews avoid being moved to the Budapest ghetto. Horthy also specifically said to her that he would not sign or approve any new anti-Jewish laws. She addresses many of the criticisms leveled at Horthy in regard to the Jewish issue, and makes an argument similar to what some historians have stated, that at the time they had to be very cautious in taking any action out of fear of German reprisal, plus not knowing who in the government to trust. She describes him not trusting his officials, and being sometimes easily misled by military reports. She later discusses the circumstances around Horthy's stopping the deportations, and addresses the question of what they knew. Bowden does not mince words when describing the horrors of the genocide, but also admits that at the time even she could not imagine the brutality and extent of Hitler's war on the Jews, giving an example that when she heard him say he would crush and exterminate them, while she was outraged, she did not take him literally, believing he was speaking in a societal and economic sense.[187]

She describes the Auschwitz Protocols as the first hard evidence of the truth amidst a sea of rumors, and that even after reading them that some aspects of the brutality of the deportations remained concealed from Horthy and his small entourage. She goes on to defend her father-in-law's record regarding the Jews, while not avoiding his statements during the 1919 counterrevolution and his approval of the early *numerus clausus* law. She emphasizes that they all had no idea that the deported Jews were being executed, and that once it was discovered Horthy protected all remaining Jews, not just the rich, a feat he was able to accomplish because by that time

---

[187] Bowden, 168-172.

the German war effort was floundering and they had fewer resources with which to challenge him. She also cites postwar statements by people close to Horthy as well as by Hungarian Jews, supporting this argument.[188]

While Horthy should not be completely absolved of responsibility for the deportation and death of so many Hungarian Jews, and he could and should have done more, the stronger case is the one that lines up with the Horthy we have seen from 1920, the one who let the early anti-Jewish laws go largely unenforced, the one who kept nearly all his country's Jews safe until 1944 when his country was occupied and he lost his freedom of action, or at least believed he had, knowing full well that his roster of supporters was dwindling. Could he have prompted serious resistance had he resigned? Possibly. Did the fact that the less desirable Jews were targeted first slow his action? Probably. But, again, had Horthy acted sooner and been removed as a result, it is just as likely that someone like Sztojay or Szalasi would have taken things to just where the Germans wanted, and overseen the extermination of every Hungarian Jew.

We must also take into account the effect the state of the German war effort had on Horthy's ability to act. Sakmyster describes Horthy as surprised at his ability to act in late June and early July, to the point that he gave serious thought to a military clash with the Germans. This, of course, was months after the occupation had begun, during which time the German war effort continued to falter, and during which time Germany's assertion of control in Hungary relaxed (as we have described elsewhere, Vessenmayer and Eichmann were caught off guard by Horthy's firm decision to stop the deportations.) It is undeniable that in this later time Horthy had more of an ability to act, the Germans less of an ability to respond quickly to stop or remove him. Had he resisted from the start, he most likely would have been removed, while at this stage he managed to hold on to power for a time. To ignore such factors, as some historians have done, is to ignore the bigger picture surrounding the events of 1944. As a matter of fact, when Horthy did act, after being presented with hard, detailed evidence about the truth of the

---

[188] Bowden, 172-175.

deportations and persuasive arguments from confidants and foreign leaders, he moved slowly, believing that too drastic a challenge would lead to the Germans swiftly stopping him. Additionally, Horthy would not have the support of significant portions of Hungarian society, making challenging the Germans all the more difficult. Again, we can only speculate on what would have transpired had Horthy resigned in protest on March 19, or resisted the German demand to deport the Jews. It is not beyond reason to argue that more lives might have been saved, that Horthy did indeed possess more power even than he believed, but it is at least as likely that doing so would have led to the deaths of even more Hungarian Jews (Veesenmayer actually made a note to postpone earlier planned deportations of Jews from Budapest, officially for logistical reasons, but likely also because taking such action in Budapest so soon would lead to petitions from the otherwise largely compliant Jewish leadership, which would reach Horthy, and possibly stir him to action.) Had Horthy resigned or mounted failed resistance early on, we might today be criticizing him for taking such a rash or symbolic action when he might have helped by staying in office.[189]

Before concluding this analysis, we must also address the more purely political events of the late Kallay period and the months of the occupation, in particular the events surrounding Horthy's failed attempt to retake control and take Hungary out of the war in October 1944. Additionally, it should be acknowledged that there was a (very small) Hungarian government presence outside of the country. It was nowhere near the scale of, say, the Polish government-in-exile, but there was a tentative plan, prior to the outbreak of the war, while Pal Teleki was still the prime minister, to form a Hungarian government in the West should Germany make aggressive moves toward Hungary. There is little information on this plan, which, due to the unexpected success of the initial Nazi *blitzkrieg* at the start of the war was never in a position to be put into action, but what we do have is a short essay by Hungary's minister in Washington, John Pelenyi, along with several preserved letters between him and the Hungarian government. What we learn

---

[189] Levai, 82-83; Sakmyster, 346-347,353-255, 360-361

from these is that as late as 1940, the pro-Western Teleki as well as Horthy both considered preparing such a plan, which only a handful of people were aware of, likely due to Teleki's awareness of the growing pro-German feelings among many officials. This is further examined in a thesis written by Brad A. Gutierrez discussing in detail precisely the reasons the Hungarian exile movement in the United States failed to produce any organized or effective results in seeking western sympathies for German-controlled Hungary, despite notable Hungarians supporting it along with the government. Ultimately, Gutierrez comes to the conclusion that the failure of this movement stemmed from several factors: an inability by Hungarian sympathizers (left-wing Hungarian émigrés and those representing the Horthy government) to work together and looking out for their own interests rather than Hungary's interests, and a lack interest by the American government during the early stages of the war, and then an unwillingness by the United States to lend support to a country that was, at least on paper, part of the Axis. But while it ultimately came to nothing, the fact that this movement existed with the support of the Horthy government as early as 1938, in secret, reinforces the argument that the first choice of Horthy and his confidants was to remain in the good graces of the western world.[190]

Part 6: Horthy's Final Maneuvers

By the late summer of 1944, Horthy's mind was made up, and he resolved to find a way out of the war even if it meant giving in to the demands of the hated Soviets. By late September, an agreement was arranged, and Horthy and his associates sought to find the right time to pull out of the war and change sides. Again, however, German intelligence was aware of the plans and began to support Ferenc Szalasi's Arrow Cross Party to thwart Horthy's plan.

---

[190] John Pelenyi, "The Secret Plan for a Hungarian Government in the West at the Outbreak of World War II," *Journal of Modern History*, 36, no. 2 (1964): 170-177; Brad A. Gutierrez, "The Hungarian Exile Movement in the United States During World War II and the American Response," (Master's thesis, Indiana University, 1995), 1-2, 44-45.

Informed of this, Horthy decided that the only course of action was to announce the armistice earlier than planned in order to avoid an Arrow Cross coup. However, this left too little time for his own military preparations. On October 15, 1944, Horthy made a radio proclamation announcing the move, but his forces were not prepared, and the Germans were. Otto Skorzeny's SS commando unit, already in Budapest, kidnapped and transported to the Dachau concentration camp Horthy's only remaining child, Miklos[191] and seized control of Budapest, with Horthy's loyalists only in tenuous control of the royal palace. By the next day, Horthy was a prisoner of the Germans, and was blackmailed by Veesenmayer into appointing Szalasi prime minister, and recant his proclamation from the previous day, with his son Miklos used as leverage. Horthy and his family were then taken to Germany, where they were held for the remainder of the war. Under Arrow Cross rule, conditions in Hungary further deteriorated, with the Jews bearing the brunt of it, until the Soviets occupied the country in the spring of 1945.[192]

We have already discussed Horthy's assertion of authority as it pertains to the Jewish issue, but his attempt to reclaim control over Hungary's future went beyond that. This story both demonstrates that once again that Horthy and his political allies sought to push back against German control, and that, unfortunately for them, many Hungarians, especially those in high ranking political and military positions, differed in their ideology, thus bringing about the failure of Horthy's plans.

While Horthy remains the central figure in this drama, another man, General Geza Lakatos, shares center stage. Without the possibility of returning former prime minister Miklos Kallay to the position, Horthy turned to Lakatos, both because he trusted him and because it would be easier to justify appointing a general as prime minister to the Germans. Lakatos, a career military man, had met Horthy several times in the past, and was known as a more moderate military figure. In his memoir, Lakatos criticizes the

---

[191] Horthy's oldest son, Istvan, died in a plane crash while serving with the Hungarian Air Force in 1942, and his two daughters had died of disease during the interwar years.
[192] Ormos, 264-267; Romsics, 211-214; Deak, 38-40; Macartney, 234-235.

former chief of staff General Werth, relating conversations in which Werth made his pro-German feelings clear. During the war, Lakatos served on the Russian front from shortly after the declaration of war until his recall after the German occupation, as Horthy from the outset sought to appoint him to at least a cabinet position. That Lakatos's political views aligned with conservatives like Bethlen is clear both from his writings, in which he is very critical of the decision to declare war on the Soviet Union as well as the way the war was run, and from his actions while prime minister.[193]

Horthy twice attempted to appoint Lakatos to a cabinet position but was forced to back down in the face of both German and Arrow Cross pressure, and was made to appoint others who were more pro-German. During this period Szalasi and his Arrow Cross forcibly inserted themselves more and more into politics, and in the spring Szalasi met with Horthy and tried to convince him to enter into an alliance with the Arrow Cross and other Hungarist movements. Horthy refused, which once again demonstrates his committed opposition to the truly radical right. Had he come to an arrangement with Szalasi, even with some compromises on the latter's part, Horthy would have most likely remained in power throughout the war and would have enjoyed widespread support from the Arrow Cross which, despite no longer being at its peak size and thus not an imminent coup threat, was able to punch above its weight after the occupation [194]

That Horthy chose to push forward and appoint a government, which, in his words, would be made up of "civil servants," in essence military officers, around the same time that he intervened to save the Jews of Budapest is no coincidence, as another development surrounding the pending deportation gave him cause to worry. In the days leading up to the planned deportation of Budapest's Jews, a large concentration of gendarmes under the command

---

[193] Geza Lakatos, *As I Saw It: The Tragedy of Hungary* trans. Mario Fenyo (Englewood, NJ: Universe Publishing Company, 1993), 34-35, 41-49.

[194] Lakatos, 102-109; Sakmyster, 341-342, 354-355; Gyorgy Ranki, "The Problem of Fascism in Hungary," in *Native Fascism in the Successor States, 1918-1945,* ed. Peter F. Sugar (Santa Barbara, CA: American Bibliographical Center—Clio Press, 1971), 71.

of Baky (who, at that time, Horthy had already requested be relived) appeared in Budapest. These gendarmes, which were at least as influenced by the far right as the army, if not more so, were perceived as a coup threat, coordinated by the Gestapo. In response, Horthy had them ordered out of the city, and also called in a few loyal military units. Despite arguments by the chief of staff, General Janos Voros, that there was no plot afoot and that taking an action like this would invite further German intervention, Horthy pressed on, and ordered his loyal forces to remove the gendarmes from the city and moved to relieve Baky and Endre of their duties. For several days there was a tense waiting game, as the risk of German intervention was great. However, Horthy had managed to catch the Germans off guard and they were unprepared to stop him—one could also argue that he got lucky—and thus Sztojay consented to heed Horthy. Baky and Endre were removed, the gendarmes withdrawn, and the deportations stopped. Horthy also took advantage of his loyal military presence in the city to station soldiers at key locations without informing Voros, thus setting up the conditions to appoint a new military government—though not a military dictatorship.[195]

Over the next few weeks, Horthy would make the case to the Germans that the Sztojay government had been ineffective and corrupt, and that he planned to eliminate political parties and appoint a military government. By the end of August, further buoyed by Bulgaria and Romania's defection to the Allies, Horthy succeeded in appointing Lakatos prime minister, though compromises were made through negotiations with Veesenmayer regarding cabinet positions.[196]

With this victory, however, Horthy, Lakatos, and their allies were in a very precarious situation. It was clear that the war was going to end before too long, with a German defeat. Especially in light of Bulgaria and Romania abandoning the Axis, and the ominously approaching Soviet army, finding a way out of the war—preferably surrendering to the western Allies rather than the Soviets—became a priority. As mentioned above, attempts to make a deal with the western Allies were made prior to the occupation, but had gotten

---

[195] Fenyo, 203-205; Sakmyster, 351-353; Lakatos, 103.
[196] Sakmyster, 360-361; Montgomery, 196-197; Lakatos, 110-115.

nowhere. By this point, the chances of doing so were even slimmer, and the only option would be to negotiate with the Soviets. Understandably, this was not ideal for Horthy, who had risen to power on a wave of anti-communist feeling, and during the interwar years had been one of the foremost anti-communist crusaders. As a result, for the next two months, he and his advisors continued to hope for an option that did not involve surrender to and occupation by the Soviets, rather a joint occupation, provided that the Soviets could be held off. There is also Horthy's archaic sense of honor to consider; he was loathe to act in a manner that would be considered a "betrayal" of Germany, as much as he had come to despise it. Ideally, that would mean informing Germany what Hungary was planning, and giving Germans forces a chance to withdraw. One component of this plan, interestingly, was to actually demand from Hitler additional forces to aid in the defense against the Soviets. This would theoretically serve two goals; if granted, the forces could potentially hold long enough to allow the western Allies to enter Hungary, thus ensuring a joint occupation, and if refused, it could be used to say that Germany was not being a faithful ally, justifying Hungary's pulling out of the war.[197]

However, as before, there was another problem that Horthy, Lakatos, Bethlen (who had managed to sneak back into the palace), and the rest of his small circle had to face: opposition from the significant pro-German forces in Hungary's army and government. In a crown council vote in late September concerning an armistice, there was a great deal of division. Many of the ministers, as well as army officers, still believed in an eventual German victory. Even among his loyal circle there was division, with Bethlen in favor of going around the crown council, given that its pro-German members would surely report to Veesenmayer on the armistice proposal. Others, like Lakatos, disagreed, arguing that the cabinet had to be involved. Eventually, it was decided that the cabinet would simply be informed that Horthy had made a final decision. However, Bethlen's worries proved true, and in the cabinet meeting the measure was unanimously opposed; Lakatos, in his memoir,

---

[197] Fenyo, 206-210; Sakmyster, 360-365; Horthy, 274-276; Lakatos, 128-129.

credits a strong argument by the minister of the interior with swaying the vote. Lakatos then had the unhappy duty of returning to Horthy with the cabinet's offer of resignation. Horthy, extremely distraught that even the ministers most loyal to him had sided against him, told Lakatos that he would bow to the cabinet's decision and remain in the war. However, he hinted that he would still use his authority to explore other options, plans he revealed only to his family and a few loyal advisors. He would go around the government whenever possible, and personally take up the task of securing an armistice, even if it had to be with the Soviets.[198]

As some of Horthy's primary confidants at this time were family, Bowden's account is extremely useful in understanding what was taking place, as she was present at nearly all of his secret meetings. In what appears to be an honest accounting, Bowden relates her frustrations with both Horthy's insistence on disclosing actions to the Germans—her logic being that Horthy had no obligation to be honest when the Germans had not been so—as well as with the reluctance of the ministers, including Lakatos, to accept that they would have to seek an armistice with the Soviets immediately. Drawing also on the writings of General Antal Vattay, she describes the initial contacts with Soviet representatives, as well as a final attempt to communicate with the British, through a British officer who had escaped into Hungary from a German POW camp. Unfortunately, the mission, which involved smuggling him and a few others out of the country by airplane, led to nothing due to logistical and communication errors, plus a lack of interest by the British.[199]

We also gain more insight from Istvan Szent-Miklosy's book, *With the Hungarian Independence Movement: An Eyewitness Account*, in which he describes his extensive involvement with what was known as the Hungarian Independence Movement, as well as Miklos Horthy Jr.'s "Breakaway Group." More importantly, both of these accounts underscore the extreme secrecy that went into these plans, that there was a very real risk of German sympathizers—or German surveillance itself—finding out. These negotiations with Soviet representatives continued until literally the days

---

[198] Lakatos, 135-136; Sakmyster, 365
[199] Bowden, 194-195, 198-202

before Horthy's fateful public broadcast, during which time Bowden was given the task of decoding communications, working closely with Horthy's son, Miklos. Despite all the attempts at secrecy, however, evidence suggests that the Germans were aware of something being planned, if not what, as German planes would be heard every time the palace's secret radio was used. However, at this point we start to see some of the problems that would ultimately lead to failure, namely indecisiveness and poor communication. For example, one plan called for Horthy and his family to travel north, to the city of Huszt, where they could be under the protection of the First Army, commanded by the loyal General Bela Miklos. However, just days before they were due to leave, the trip was cancelled. Horthy claimed that the chief of general staff, General Voros, thought the move too risky, but Bowden writes that in Voros's memoir, he stated that it was Horthy who cancelled the trip. Whether this was a miscommunication, or a disagreement between the two, it is emblematic of the problems facing the Horthy regime in its final days.[200]

By October 11, after many back and forth communications, a preliminary armistice agreement with the Soviets was authorized by Horthy for signing by his representatives in Moscow. This agreement represented Horthy swallowing his pride yet again, as he agreed to rather severe terms that he had previously tried to negotiate down. With the news of rapidly advancing Soviet forces, and learning that the Germans were prepared to abandon most of Hungary to the Soviets anyway—a development which convinced even the previously skeptical advisors such as Lakatos and Voros that the time had come to get out of the war. Once the document was signed, the Soviets took on a friendlier attitude, and Foreign Minister Vyacheslav Molotov agreed to a temporary, unannounced truce at the front to allow Horthy time to make arrangements for the defection and surrender. Stalin even seemed to be leaning toward letting Horthy remain Hungary's head of state in the transitional government. However, as Sakmyster points out, despite Horthy's remarkable success in formulating and negotiating the armistice, he would

---

[200] Istvan Szent-Miklosy, *With the Hungarian Independence Movement: An Eyewitness Account* (New York: Praeger Publishers, 1988), 49-55; Bowden, 209-211; Fenyo, 224-226.

fare far worse when it came to executing the agreement.[201]

Initially, Horthy planned the defection for October 20, and still intended on informing the Germans of his intentions prior to that. Additionally, the commanders of Hungary's armed forces would be ordered to cease hostilities with the Soviets, and troops would be withdrawn to Budapest to retain control of the city should the Germans attempt to take it by force. There were several problems with this plan. First, he severely overestimated the level of support for him within the armed forces, and thus saw no reason to arm workers' groups and others to spark a national resistance. Second, he failed to properly recognize just how many Hungarians, from the middle class to the army to his own cabinet, had completely thrown in their lot with the Germans, choosing, as Horthy himself might have years earlier, to fall alongside the Germans rather than accept communist domination of the country. Third, Horthy did not attempt to flee Budapest and announce the defection from a safer location with the army. Sakmyster adds that while the Germans did not know of the communications with Moscow—an admittedly impressive feat for Horthy and his supporters—they had thoroughly prepared for a betrayal by Horthy, with Veesenmayer even coordinating with Szalasi and the Arrow Cross, something the Germans had not been keen on doing earlier, as they held a low opinion of the Hungarian fascists.[202]

Indeed, Szent-Miklosy writes that starting in early October the Arrow Cross grew far bolder, and efforts to clamp down on it failed, with their leaders even escaping arrest thanks to German help. Szent-Miklosy, who had previously been involved with the military, also provides some specific examples showing that Horthy's trust in many of these officer was misplaced. The Arrow Cross actions, taken with open German support, became so great that there was a fear that a coup was being planned, something which in part prompted Horthy to declare the armistice several days earlier than planned.[203]

In his memoir, Horthy writes that he based his decision on the assumption that the Germans were aware of his plan, and were preparing to depose him

---

[201] Horthy, 277-284; Sakmyster, 368-369.
[202] Sakmyster, 369-371.
[203] Szent-Miklosy, 150-156; Sakmyster, 371-372; Bowden, 214-217.

by force and appoint Szalasi as head of state. Horthy reasoned that the only way to counter this was to move up the date of the declaration of the armistice, in the hope that he would catch the Germans and their supporters off guard. So, at noon on October 15, he met with Veesenmayer, informed him of his intentions, and went ahead with his radio broadcast. This decision was opposed by Lakatos and Voros, both of whom noted that the preparations were not complete, and that they could not guarantee the loyalty of the army officers. Horthy also refused to make the declaration from a more secure location, invoking the naval maxim that a captain never abandon his ship, despite warnings that if he remained in the palace he would be captured in hours. The final event that ensured both the early implementation of the plan as well as its failure was the abduction of Horthy's son by the infamous Otto Skorzeny. Lured out of the palace on the pretense of meeting with representatives of Yugoslavia's Josip Broz Tito, but betrayed by a German spy in his inner circle, the young Horthy was quickly captured. Additionally, days earlier the commander of the loyal army forces in Budapest, General Szilard Bakay, had been kidnapped by the Germans. With no other option, however, Horthy went ahead and made the proclamation over the radio. Very soon after, the radio station was captured, and Horthy's orders countermanded. The largely pro-German military happily complied. To Horthy's dismay, only his personal guard at the palace put up a brief fight against overwhelming German forces.[204]

All in all, it was a complete failure on all levels, though some historians have argued that Horthy designed it to fail in order to maintain his alliance with the Germans to the end. However, there is very little evidence to support this claim and the primary sources do not support this theory. Both Lakatos and Bowden, who were in close contact with Horthy on the 15th and beyond make this clear. Lakatos describes the scene in the crown council where the cabinet was finally informed of the armistice plan, and describes the pro-German ministers as being caught completely by surprise. Horthy personally notes Veesenmayer's shock. Lakatos also describes the confusion within the

---

[204] Sakmyster, 371-373; Kertesz, 82-82; Horthy, 287-289; Montgomery, 198-199.

military, caught off guard and the loyalist elements hopelessly outnumbered—the new commander of the forces in Budapest was arrested by his subordinate. Beyond that, General Voros was convinced by Veesenmayer to countermand Horthy's orders to stop fighting the Soviets.[205]

Bowden, with her closer view of things, describes Horthy's reaction to the developments. Regarding the kidnapping of his son—who, she writes, had not been supposed to leave the safety of the palace—Horthy was visibly shaken, and in his meeting with Veesenmayer prior to the proclamation angrily confronted him regarding the kidnapping. Bowden is also critical of Lakatos, who she sees as having been overly cautious, having altered some phrases in Horthy's declaration he deemed to harsh, but in his doing so Bowden writes that the message became less clear, leading to confusion regarding the armistice. Lakatos writes that he did so because he felt it too dangerous to take a harsh tone when they were in a weak position. Bowden also relates an additional betrayal by another military officer, who instructed that orders from the palace should not be transmitted to the armed forces, and calls out General Voros's double-dealing. She further criticizes Lakatos regarding his decision to open contacts with the Germans, who were demanding the removal of mines placed around the Castle Hill complex, which trapped the German embassy and the Arrow Cross leaders. In his memoir, Lakatos describes negotiating for the release of Miklos Horthy Jr. and General Bakay, and that the mines were not useful against the Germans, so he did not fight over them. Bowden disputes this. She also describes, later, talking with Vattay regarding a deal with the Germans, Horthy having apparently refused to consider handing over power in exchange for asylum for his family. She echoed his refusal. Eventually, however, after the family (apart from Horthy) had sought refuge at the residence of the Papal Nuncio, they learned that Horthy had apparently consented to be taken to Germany.[206]

In an ironic end to this saga, there was yet another communication failure within Horthy's group as Lakatos had told the Germans that Horthy had agreed to the deal, having been informed of this by Vattay. However, both

---

[205] Fenyo, 228-229; Lakatos, 164-169.
[206] Bowden, 219-223, 226-234, 239-243; Lakatos, 166-167.

Horthy and Bowden deny that he ever communicated such a decision. The only rationalization they were able to make was that the previously loyal officer had done so in an attempt to save the lives of Horthy and his family. The decision made for him, all that remained was to officialize it. After twice curtly refusing to appoint Szalasi prime minister (Szalasi personally came to request this), Horthy was presented with a document that concluded with a printed, "Signed, Horthy." After some back and forth, after which it became clear that whether or not he signed, it would be published as if he had signed it, Horthy begrudgingly signed it after securing a promise that his son would be released safely, though he notes in his memoir that it cannot have been considered legal, having been signed under duress.[207] In his own writings, Lakatos also states that he never officially resigned as prime minister. This done, Szalasi and his Arrow Cross, which had already *de facto* seized power, had a shred of legitimacy to claim as they began a short period of rule that terrorized Budapest's remaining Jews.[208]

Regarding Horthy's final act as regent, it is possible to fault him for signing the German document at all, granting Szalasi some form of legitimacy, especially knowing that it would be publicized that he signed regardless. However, before assigning blame the situation must be understood. His plan to leave the war had failed completely, his last son was missing, possibly in danger of death, and he was under constant pressure by the Germans, Arrow Cross, and some of his own entourage to surrender and hand over power (surrendering having been done in his name without even asking him). Furthermore, the rest of his family was possibly in danger, and as they were held in the palace, his longtime ally and aide-de-camp, Gyuszi Tost, committed suicide. The amount of pressures on a then 76 year old man, after weeks of planning the action, cannot be underestimated. Plus, he likely rationalized that since it would be announced that he had signed over power

---

[207] This promise was not kept, and Miklos Horthy Jr. remained in the Dachau concentration camp until the war's end, when he was finally reunited with his family.

[208] Horthy, 290-295; Bowden, 238-245; Lakatos, 171-172, 174-185; Szent-Miklosy, 68-69.

anyway, he decided that signing it for real, under protest, in exchange for the promise of his son's safety was fair (he apparently did not consider how it would look to history.) He would term that day "the saddest day of my life." In the end, the Horthy era ended much like it began, with a chaotic coup, and a leader arguably in over his head, pulled in multiple directions, leading a nation steadily drifting further and further right.[209]

---

[209] Fenyo, 236-238; Horthy, 292-294; Sakmyster, 379-380; Bowden, 246.

CONCLUSION

The Admiral's Legacy

Thomas Sakmyster puts it best when he describes the Horthy era as a collection of paradoxes and ironies. In addition to the ironies of Horthy himself, an admiral without a navy, the ruler of a monarchy without a king, Hungary the country itself exhibited paradoxes. It was the first country in Europe to pass antisemitic legislation, yet, during World War II, it was one of the last places considered safe for Jews in Hitler-dominated Europe, a nation led by a self-professed antisemite. Horthy's Hungary was possibly the most ardent anti-communist nation for most of the interwar period, and yet by 1944 Horthy was willing to unconditionally surrender to the archenemy, Stalin. Many of Hungary's political elite identified more strongly with the West, even while allied with Nazi Germany. While Horthy was, for most of his time as Regent, a fair head of state, letting more experienced politicians manage affairs of state and presiding over Hungary's recovery from its dismemberment after World War I, he was in many respects a poor leader, and open to being influenced by those around him. When those people were members of the far right, as in the early years of his reign, he drifted in that direction, eventually settling with the more moderate conservative right-wing ideology espoused by aristocratic elites, such as Istvan Bethlen.[210]

However, therein lay the problem. While much of the political elite, preferring to keep things as close to the old status quo as possible, maintained

---

[210] Sakmyster, *v-vii*, 397-400.

more moderate positions, many Magyars embraced the more "modern"
radical right-wing ideology. There were multiple factors to this shift,
including the trauma of Trianon and Bela Kun's short-lived communist
regime, and a significant German minority which, after Hitler's rise to power,
largely embraced Nazi ideology and brought it to Hungary's military, where
they were prominently placed. However, fault also lies in Horthy who, while
part of the counterrevolution (along with future leaders of Hungary's far
right), made inflammatory statements regarding Jews, communists, and
territorial revision, all of which served to inflame the populace and eventually
move large segments of society further right than Horthy or his associates.
Additionally, the regime's emphasis on revision, and the early anti-Jewish laws
lent legitimacy to those radicals. But as we have seen, Horthy, agreeing with
his conservative advisors, moved away from the more radical side of the
Hungarian right, which later put him at odds with both the military
leadership and several of his prime ministers.[211]

This, of course, came to a head in 1944, with the German occupation,
and the pro-German government Horthy was forced to appoint. While we
have discussed to what degree Horthy was culpable in what happened to
Hungary's Jews during this time, as well as his positive actions in July of 1944,
we have also seen the extreme level of collaboration by many Hungarians, in
particular the gendarmes and the military, who later came into conflict with
Horthy and contributed to the ultimate failure of his attempt to steer
Hungary out of the war. By this point, Horthy was incapable of changing
Hungary's trajectory, having become part of an elite minority which, while it
held power, did not represent the people.

It is not uncommon today, given the level of reverence held for Horthy by
Hungary's far-right Jobbik, for any analysis that is more lenient than the
standard liberal/left-wing view to be labeled an attempt to "rehabilitate"
Horthy, to downplay the bad that occurred under his stewardship. However,
such an attitude contributes to a poorer understanding of the Horthy era, as
Horthy cannot be treated in the same manner as a Mussolini or a Hitler.

[211] Sakmyster, 383-386.

While, as mentioned, Horthy did contribute to the rise of the far right, for much of his reign, acting against national trends, he was an adversary of the far right, and openly voiced his disgust with Szalasi and the Arrow Cross. The fact is that the general mood of Hungarians was shifting rightward with or without Horthy by the 1930s, which is why Horthy, along with the known anglophile Pal Teleki, worked to try and "take the wind out of the sails" of the far right to maintain political control while not giving in to the radical demands.

If Horthy is to be blamed for the events of 1944 in a substantive manner, he should be blamed for his weakness in the face of the German occupation, his indecisiveness when separated from his advisors, his slowness to act on the deportations, and being far too trusting of military officers and officials appointed to government posts, despite having already seen examples of such people being untrustworthy and despicable.[212]

To address the question of Horthy's legacy, both of the main viewpoints we see represented in today's controversies are incorrect. Horthy does not deserve statues and busts in public places in Hungary, as Jobbik believes, but neither can he be termed simply a "Hitler ally," as opponents of Jobbik state. He was a flawed man and a very flawed leader, but one who could have succeeded as a head of state should Europe have remained peaceful, as evidenced by Hungary's recovery during the 1920s under Prime Minister Bethlen. Despite some instances of cleverness in dealing with the Germans, Horthy was politically inept, prone to being swayed by strong arguments and his own passions, and had trouble making decisions without consulting advisors beforehand.

At the same time, however, his virtues and old-world sense of honor cannot be ignored. Despite declaring himself an antisemite, he never subscribed to the murderous sort of antisemitism seen in the far right movements, and he did put a stop to the deportations, saving 200,000 Jews in Budapest, in the only instance during the war that armed forces of a German ally were used to save Jews. He also maintained Hungary's neutrality

---

[212] Hanebrink, 195-198.

at the start of the war, allowing many Polish refugees to pass through to the Allies, and later on was a very reluctant ally of Germany before he attempted to leave the war entirely.

This clearly shows the difference between Horthy, his supporters, and much of the country. Had he wanted to ensure popular support, it would have been very easy for Horthy to gain the support of the far right by embracing its ideology, throwing Hungary fully into cooperation with Germany. Ultimately, to use another naval metaphor, Horthy, the captain, and much of the people, his crew, were at odds, and with neither side willing to change, it was not going to end well, and Horthy was never adept enough to effectively stymie the far right. The divide became too great, too quickly.

As the far right rises again in Hungary today, it is more important to understand what happened last time, as the same Christian nationalist sentiments that drove the movement then are driving Jobbik today, and Prime Minister Viktor Orban's Fidesz party occupies a similar position to Horthy's administration. Orban is right wing, and engages in Christian Nationalist rhetoric at times, but, for now, remains distinct and less radical. One can even make the argument that the controversy over Horthy's legacy today is a continuation of some of the conflict we saw during the interwar years. After the war, Hungary became a communist state, and the right was broadly demonized and repressed. Now, over 20 years after the fall of the Soviet Union and Hungary's emergence from behind the iron curtain, Hungarian nationalism has reasserted itself in a not dissimilar manner to the reaction against Bela Kun's communist regime (minus the violent counterrevolution, of course). Additionally, today the right in Hungary has the enemies it can rally people against: Muslim immigration and the European Union. As in the 1920s, there is anger directed at the perceived threats of non-Christian, non-Magyar elements changing Hungarian society, and an international community that is seen as having wronged the country. The biggest difference in modern Hungary can be seen by the reactions to the statues and busts of Horthy and other figures from interwar Hungary. Hungary today is a democracy, and while it remains a more conservative society than Western European nations, it certainly allows more political freedom than Horthy's

Hungary—you would not have been likely to see a protest like the defacement of a statue of Horthy in 2012.

To focus our understanding of the Horthy era on a handful of controversial points rather than understanding what happened in Hungarian society at the time, and how it impacted the power structure, is to prevent ourselves from properly understanding and dealing with politics in modern Hungary. As much as we might be critical of Jobbik, its members' grievances come from real places, and they have to be addressed—but in a manner within the rule of law, and in a reasonable way, not allowing a fringe group to dictate policy while still addressing the legitimate concerns of the people and maintaining unity between all of Hungary's residents. The largest long-term failing of the Horthy regime was that its elites' primary goal was to restore and maintain the old status quo as much as possible, in a period where, as we have seen, most people did not want it. However, such a statement is made with the benefit of both hindsight and modern values, and even still it is hard to state exactly how Horthy and his close associates could have maintained a unified, moderate nation when so much of Hungary's populace was inclined rightward, due to events that had taken place before Horthy was appointed regent.

Today, as has been mentioned, Hungary is in a better position to maintain order. Prime Minister Orban has not ignored the main grievances of the new far right, defying the EU and actively preventing additional migrants from entering the country. In doing so, he is "taking the wind out of the sails" of the far right in a similar manner to what Horthy and his allies did, and has even stated that he aims to make Hungary into an "illiberal democracy," something which sounds reminiscent of Horthy's Hungary, where there was general freedom but still repression of extreme political views on both ends of the spectrum, which has led to him being harshly criticized by everyone to his left.[213]

To conclude by returning to Horthy's legacy, and the protests surrounding

---

[213] Attila Mong, "Is Hungary's Leader Giving Up on Europe?" Foreignpolicy.com, April 18, 2016, http://foreignpolicy.com/2016/04/18/is-hungarys-leader-giving-up-on-europe-eu-european-union-orban/.

it, we see a significant divide in the arguments put forward by both sides. Anti-Horthy protestors only bring up the period of Nazi occupation, while those in support demonstrate much more knowledge of the Horthy period, bringing up Hungary's recovery under his rule, and pointing out that he was not tried at Nuremburg, though they minimize his negative choices.[214] Again, this is not to say that Horthy necessarily deserves statues; there is certainly what to criticize regarding both him and his administration, though at the same time there is not a strong argument as to why, in a country with statues of many historical figures, a flawed but important statesman cannot be represented. Regarding modern Hungary, which is still recovering from economic recession (another parallel with part of the Horthy era), and seeing a rise in hatred of minority groups in the face of a legitimate existential threat, it is important for people to understand that the Horthy era was more than World War II, and that the regime, however repressive, was in fact preventing the actual far right from controlling Hungary's trajectory. There are lessons to be learned from the successes and failures of the Horthy regime, what it can be held accountable for and what it cannot be. Defacing statues and focusing on only one piece of Horthy's legacy will only further divide the nation and energize the most radical elements of the right. Only by properly understanding the man that Jobbik and others idolize can a reasoned discussion about him be had, and only reasoned discussion between the opposing sides can ensure that Hungary does not make any of the same mistakes it made from the end of the First World War to the end of the Second World War—as well as ensuring that Hungary continues to endure and serve as a defender of modern Europe. Both sides may be surprised at what they find.

---

[214] Marton Dunai, "Hungary's Far-Right Jobbik Honours Nazi-Linked Wartime Leader Miklos Horthy," smh.com/au, November 4, 2013, http://www.smh.com.au/world/hungarys-farright-jobbik-honours-nazilinked-wartime-leader-miklos-horthy-20131103-2wva5.html.

Bibliography

Primary Sources

"Banffy Defends Restriction of Jewish Admissions," Jta.com. January 2, 1923. http://www.jta.org/1923/01/02/archive/banffy-defends-restriction-of-jewish-admissions.

"Bethlen Reported to Have Decided on More Liberal Jewish Policy," Jta.org. March 6, 1924. http://www.jta.org/1924/03/06/archive/bethlen-reported-to-have-decided-on-more-liberal-jewish-policy.

Bowden, Ilona. *Honour and Duty: The Memoirs of Countess Ilona Edelsheim Gyulai Widow of Stephen Horthy, Vice-regent of Hungary.* Lewes, UK: Purple Pagoda Press Ltd, 2005.

Horthy, Miklos, and Andrew L. Simon. *Admiral Nicholas Horthy: Memoirs.* Safety Harbor, FL: Simon Publications, 2000.

Jazsi, Oscar. *Revolution and Counter-Revolution in Hungary.* New York: H. Fertig, 1969.

Kallay, Miklos. *Hungarian Premier: A Personal Account of a Nation's Struggle in the Second World War.* New York: Columbia University Press, 1954.

Lakatos, Geza. *As I Saw it: The Tragedy of Hungary*. Translated by Mario D. Fenyo. Englewood, NJ: Universe Publishing Company, 1993.

Montgomery, John Flournoy. *Hungary: The Unwilling Satellite*. Morristown, NJ: Vista Books, 1993.

"Numerus Clausus Will not Be Repealed in Hungary Until Lost Provinces Are Restored, Minister of Education Says," Jta.org. June 11 1924. http://www.jta.org/1924/06/11/archive/numerus-clausus-will-not-be-repealed-in-hungary-until-lost-provinces-are-restored-minister-of-educa.

"Rothschilds, Kuhn Loeb & Co. Assailed for Aiding Hungary," Jta.org. May 17, 1923. http://www.jta.org/1923/05/17/archive/rothschilds-kuhn-loeb-co-assailed-for-aiding-Hungary.

Soros, Tivadar. *Masquerade: Dancing Around Death in Nazi-Occupied Hungary*. Translated by Humphrey Tonkin. New York: Arcade Publishing, 2001.

Szent-Miklosy, Istvan. *With the Hungarian Independence Movement: An Eyewitness Account*. New York: Praeger Publishers, 1988.

Szinai, Miklos, and Laszlo Szucs. *The Confidential Papers of Admiral Horthy*. Budapest: Corvina Press, 1965.

Tepesblog, Vlad. "Orban's Historic Speech Puts Hungary on War Footing." Youtube video, 13:02. March 18 2016. https://www.youtube.com/watch?v=EbINrdyAXlE.

Zsolt, Bela. *Nine Suitcases: A Memoir*. New York: Schocken Books, 2004.

Secondary Sources

Barany, George. "The Dragon's Teeth: The Roots of Hungarian Fascism."
In *Native Fascism in the Successor States, 1918-1945,* edited by Peter F.
Sugar, 73-82. Santa Barbara, California: American Bibliographical Center—
Clio Press, 1971.

Braham, Randolph L. *Politics of Genocide : The Holocaust in Hungary,
Condensed Edition.* Detroit: Wayne State University Press, 2000.

_____. "Hungary and the Holocaust: The Nationalist Drive to Whitewash
the Past." In *The Treatment of the Holocaust in Hungary and Romania
During the Post- Communist Era*, edited by Randolph L. Braham, 1-42.
Boulder, CO: The Rosenthal Institute for Holocaust Studies Graduate
Center/City University of New York and Social Science Monographs, 2004.

_____, and William J. vanden Heuvel, eds. *The Auschwitz Reports and the
Holocaust in Hungary.* Boulder, CO: Social Science Monographs, 2011.

Benziger, Karl P. "The Trial of Laszlo Bardossy. The Second World War
and Factional Politics in Contemporary Hungary." *Journal of Contemporary
History,* 40, no. 3 (2005): 465-481.

Bodo, Bela. "Hungarian Aristocracy and the White Terror." *Journal of
Contemporary History,* 45, no. 4 (2010): 703-724.

_____. "Paramilitary Violence in Hungary After the First World War."
Eastern European Quarterly 38, no. 2 (2004).

Case, Holly. *Between States: The Transylvanian Question and the European
Idea during World War II.* Stanford, CA: Stanford University Press, 2013.

Deák, Istvàn. *Hungary from 1918 to 1945.* New York: Columbia University, Institute on East Central Europe, 198

_____. "Hungary." In *The European Right: A Historical Profile.* Edited by Hans Rogger and Eugen Weber, 364-407. Berkeley: University of California Press, 1965.

_____. "A Fatal Compromise? The Debate Over Collaboration and Resistance in Hungary." *East European Politics and Societies,* 9, no. 2 (1995): 209-233.

Dreisziger, N. F. "Miklos Horthy and the Second World War: Some Historiographical Perspectives." *Hungarian Studies Review,* XXIII, no. 1 (Spring 1996): 5-16.

_____. "Contradictory Evidence Concerning Hungary's Declaration of War on the USSR in June 1941." *Canadian Slavonic Papers,* 19, no. 4 (1977): 481-488.

_____. *Hungary's Way to World War II.* Astor Park, Florida: Danubian Press Inc, 1968.

Dunai, Marton. "Hungary's Far-Right Jobbik Honours Nazi-Linked Wartime Leader Miklos Horthy." Smh.com/au. November 4, 2013. http://www.smh.com.au/world/hungarys-farright-jobbik-honours-nazilinked-wartime-leader-miklos-horthy-20131103-2wva5.html.

Fenyo, Mario D. *Hitler, Horthy, and Hungary: German-Hungarian Relations, 1941- 1944.* New Haven and London: Yale University Press, 1972.

Gutierrez, Brad A. "The Hungarian Exile Movement in the United States During World War II and the American Response." Master's thesis, Indiana University, 1995.

Hajdu, Tibor. "Transformations of the Officer Corps in Hungary." *Historical Social Research* 33, no. 2 (2008): 214-220.

Hanebrink, Paul A. *In Defense of Christian Hungary: Religion, Nationalism, and Antisemitism, 1890-1944*. Ithaca, NY: Cornell University Press, 2006.

Kertesz, Stephen D. *Diplomacy in a Whirlpool: Hungary Between Nazi Germany and Soviet Russia*. Notre Dame, IN: University of Notre Dame Press, 1953.

Kovacs, Maria M. "The Ideology of Illiberalism in the Professions: Leftist and Rightist Radicalism Among Hungarian Doctors, Lawyers and Engineers, 1918-1945." *European History Quarterly 21*, no. 2 (1991): 185-207.

Levai, Jeno, ed. *Eichmann in Hungary: Documents*. New York: Howard Fertig, 1987.

Lorman, Thomas. *Counter-Revolutionary Hungary, 1920-1925: Istvan Bethlen and the Politics of Consolidation*. Boulder, CO: East European Monographs, 2006.

Macartney, C. A. *Hungary: A Short History*. Edinburgh: The Edinburgh University Press, 1962.

Marianne Kunnen-Jones. "George B. Rieveschl Jr. Award for Scholarly or Creative Works: The Historian Who Came in From the Cold." University of Cincinnati, last modified May 19, 2000. http://www.uc.edu/profiles/sakmyst.htm.

Mendelsohn, Ezra. *The Jews of East Central Europe Between the World Wars*. Bloomington: Indiana University Press, 1983.

Mong, Attila. "Is Hungary's Leader Giving Up on Europe?" Foreignpolicy.com. April 18, 2016. http://foreignpolicy.com/2016/04/18/is-hungarys-leader-giving-up-on-europe-eu-european-union-orban/.

Ormos, Maria. "The Horthy Era and the Fascist Epilogue." In *Hungary: Governments and Politics 1848-2000,* edited by Maria Ormos and Bela K. Kiraly, translated by Nora Arato, 216-274. Highland Lakes, NJ: Social Science Monographs, Boulder, CO/Atlantic Research and Publications, Inc, 2001.

Ormos, Maria. "World War and Revolutions, 1914-1919. The New State Organization, 1920-1921." In *Hungary: Governments and Politics 1848-2000,* edited by Maria Ormos and Bela K. Kiraly, translated by Nora Arato, 167-215. Highland Lakes, NJ: Social Science Monographs, Boulder, CO: Atlantic Research and Publications, Inc, 2001.

Ormos, Maria. *Hungary in the Age of the Two World Wars 1914-1945.* Translated by Brian McLean. Boulder, CO: Social Science Monographs, Highland Lakes, NJ: Atlantic Research and Publications, Inc, 2007.

Pastor, Peter. "Hungarian-Soviet Diplomatic Relations 1935-1941: A Failed Rapprochement." *Europe-Asia Studies,* 56, no. 5 (2004): 731-750.

Payne, Stanley G. *A History of Fascism, 1914-1945.* Madison: University of Wisconsin Press, 1995.

Pelenyi, John. "The Secret Plan for a Hungarian Government in the West at the Outbreak of World War II." *Journal of Modern History,* 36, no. 2 (1964): 170-177.

Ranki, Gyorgy. "The Problem of Fascism in Hungary." In *Native Fascism in the Successor States, 1918-1945,* edited by Peter F. Sugar, 65-72. Santa Barbara, CA: American Bibliographical Center—Clio Press, 1971.

Romsics, Ignac. *Hungary in the Twentieth Century.* Budapest: Corvina Books Ltd, Osiris, 1999.

Rothschild, Joseph. *East Central Europe between the Two World Wars.* Seattle: University of Washington Press, 1977.

Sakmyster, Thomas. *Hungary's Admiral on Horseback: Miklos Horthy, 1918-1944.* Boulder, CO: East European Monographs, 1994.

_____. *Hungary, the Great Powers, and the Danubian Crisis, 1936-1939.* Athens: University of Georgia Press, 1980.

_____. "Army Officers and Foreign Policy in Interwar Hungary, 1918-1941." *Journal of Contemporary History 10*, no. 1 (1975): 19-40.

Seton-Watson, Hugh. *Eastern Europe Between the Wars, 1918-1941.* Boulder, CO: Westview Press, 1986.

Sugar, Peter F. *Native Fascism in the Successor States, 1918-1945.* Santa Barbara, CA: ABC-Clio, 1971.

Vesei, Charles P. "The Image of Admiral Horthy in Historiography." Master's thesis, Indiana University, 1994.

Wallenberg, Raoul. *Letters and Dispatches, 1924-1944.* Translated by Kjersti Board. New York: Arcade Pub., 1995.

Winchester, Betty Jo. "Hungary and the 'Third Europe.'" *Slavic Review,* 32, no. 4 (1973): 741-756

About Yakov Merkin

Yakov Merkin is currently enjoying life in Haifa, Israel. He grew up in New York City where he earned both a Bachelor's and a Master's Degree in History with Honors from Queens College of the City University of New York. His academic works on the Horthy era in Hungary have been awarded the Arnold Franco Essay Prize and the Frank Merli Prize. Yakov is now focused on writing science fiction and fantasy—creating whole new worlds. His first novel, *A Greater Duty*, is available on Amazon.

Visit Yakov at http://www.yakovmerkin.com

Follow @YakovMerkin on Twitter and Gab.

Made in the USA
San Bernardino,
CA

58807437R00082